# THE FOREIGN RELATIONS OF THE NEW STATES

STUDIES IN CONTEMPORARY SOUTHEAST ASIA

# THE FOREIGN RELATIONS
# OF THE NEW STATES

## MICHAEL LEIFER

LONGMAN

Longman Australia Pty Limited
Camberwell Victoria Australia

Associated companies, branches, and representatives
throughout the world.

First published 1974

ISBN 0 582 71042 1 (Cased)
ISBN 0 582 71043 X (Limp)

Typeset by Dudley E. King Pty Ltd, Melbourne
Printed in Hong Kong by Dai Nippon Printing Co., ( Hong Kong) Ltd

# CONTENTS

# CONTENTS

# ACKNOWLEDGEMENTS

This book was suggested by Jamie Mackie whose editorial advice
has been most helpful. A substantive draft was written at 102 West
Avenue, Ithaca, where I was fortunate enough to have a room during
the latter part of 1971. The intellectual climate of the Cornell University
Modern Indonesia Project assisted my endeavours, as did
discussions with Frank Weinstein. Peggy Lush and Fernanda Pfeil
together typed the bulk of the manuscript and my wife assisted in
its completion. Any errors of opinion and fact are, of course, my own.

Michael Leifer

London, October 1972

# INTRODUCTION

In the years since the end of the Second World War, international relations within Southeast Asia have been dominated largely by the involvements of external powers. Such an experience is not novel to a region whose diverse peoples have long encountered the influence of external forces and historically have never produced a truly hegemonic power which could rival those at its periphery. The process of colonial intervention from the West confirmed the subordination of the political units of Southeast Asia, although Anglo-French accommodation sustained the formal independence of Siam. With this one exception, independent states emerged again only in the vacuum of political authority created by the impact of Japanese military intervention in the Pacific War.

After the precipitate surrender of Japan in August 1945 international relations within Southeast Asia began to assume a novel character as nationalist movements fought against attempts at restoration by some colonial powers. Concurrently, other metropolitan countries mixed realism with benevolence to concede and sponsor independence in advance of violent resistance to continued external rule. The overall process of independence within the region was piecemeal and protracted, but in terms of historical perspective it was remarkably swift. Between 1946 and 1957 the colonial powers relinquished sovereignty of the greater part of Southeast Asia. After 1957 there occurred some minor transfers and consolidation of residual *imperium*, the most recent acquisition of independence being attained by Singapore in 1965. At the time of writing, the sole vestiges of colonial rule are the Portuguese possession on the island of Timor and Britain's conduct of the foreign relations of the miniscule state of Brunei, situated on the northern coast of Borneo.

1

Today, the independent states of Southeast Asia comprise Burma, Thailand, Laos, Cambodia, the Democratic Republic of (North) Vietnam, the Republic of (South) Vietnam, Malaysia, Singapore, Indonesia, and the Philippines.

The foreign relations of these ten states fall into three categories. First, the process of gaining independence and the pattern of post-colonial settlement have involved relationships between the new states and former rulers. Such relationships have been mixed but, in some instances, they have endured well beyond the transfer of power to become more harmonious than some intra-regional associations. A second order of relationships has arisen from local reactions to great power involvements. At this level, the role of local states has been governed by their capacity for independent action; their diplomatic reactions have been far from uniform. There has evolved also with independence a third category of relationships which is essentially intra-regional and which has involved both conflict and co-operation. With the attenuation over time of the first type of relationship and the modification of the second, especially given the impact of events in Vietnam, the third pattern of intra-regional politics may be expected to assume increasing importance.

Southeast Asia remains, nonetheless, a fragmented region composed of many enfeebled states, whose internationally recognized independence is not necessarily reflected by their internal political condition. As yet, the new states, which are the subject of this enquiry, do not possess much capacity for combining limited resources in order to overcome the subordination which geography and politics has imposed on them. As a consequence, external influences can be expected to continue to play a major role.

An understanding of the foreign relations of the new states of Southeast Asia demands an awareness of all three analytic categories and the ways in which they overlap. With this in mind, the object of the following chapters will be to evaluate international relations in the region, as far as possible, from a Southeast Asian perspective.

# Chapter One

# A NEW ORDER IN SOUTHEAST ASIA

*The Collapse of the Colonial Order*
Up to the outbreak of the Pacific War, the region now known as
Southeast Asia was almost totally subject to the direct domination
of European powers and the United States. At the turn of the
twentieth century, the United States, through force of arms, had
succeeded Spanish supremacy in the Philippines, where it also
crushed a local nationalist movement. By that time the Dutch had
virtually consolidated administrative control in their East Indies
colony, while the French were dominant and secure in a *Union
Indochinoise*; acquired piecemeal through the latter half of the
nineteenth century. The possessions of the other major colonial
power were not territorially contiguous or administratively unified.
The British, following their protracted conquest of Burma, had
brought it within the orbit of the government of India, but in 1937
it was separated politically from the sub-continent to experience a
restive quasi-autonomy. British Malaya achieved territorial defi-
nition by 1909 with the transfer of provinces from Siam, but its
constitutional and administrative pattern was highly complex and
not uniform. Across the South China Sea, the nothern portion of the
island of Borneo (Sarawak, Brunei, and North Borneo) had also
fallen under the protection of the British crown. The fifth and minor
colonial power was Portugal, which preserved a vestigial position
in the eastern portion of the island of Timor.
The sole exception was Siam (Thailand). Through an adaptive
internal policy, skilful diplomatic practice and, above all, a good
measure of geopolitical advantage, this country's rulers were able to
fend off colonial rivals and to sustain a meaningful independence.
Such independence was not preserved, however, without loss of
territory to the colonial domains of France and Britain. Nonetheless,

the modernizing Siamese state enjoyed an autonomy which contrasted with the political condition of the other countries of the region. From Burma to the Philippines, political order was shaped and dominated by external forces.

There are scholars who, in reassessing the colonial record in Southeast Asia, have demonstrated that the effective consolidation of administrative control was a much more recent phenomenon than historical myth might suggest. Valid though this revisionist evaluation may be, it is less plausible in the sphere of international relations. Indeed one notable protagonist among the revisionist historians of Southeast Asia has admitted that in the case of the Indonesian archipelago '. . . one cannot avoid the impression that, though those many independent lands had not yet been annexed politically, they had been isolated internationally except in their relations with the Indies government'.[1] It was the quality of international political isolation as much as alien control which characterized the condition of Southeast Asia under colonialism. Thus, while Dutch administration, for example, was less than complete until the early years of the twentieth century, relationships between the local rulers and the Indies government had long been encapsulated within what might be described as a colonial international system.

In general, the political entities subsumed within a variety of colonial forms had relevance for the wider international system solely in terms of the overseas interests of metropolitan powers. International relations within Southeast Asia proceeded in the main between extra-regional powers who concluded agreements defining territorial spheres of interest and advantage with almost exclusive reference to themselves. With the exception of Thailand (Siam), whose freedom of international action was restricted, competence to participate in international life was denied even to those entities treated as sovereign in legal theory. This situation continued past the outbreak of hostilities in Europe which marked the beginning of the Second World War. At this juncture the political entities of Southeast Asia were, with one exception, objects of international relations. The sole indigenous subject was Thailand.

The edifice of colonial rule was rudely shattered with the spectacular military victory of the Japanese during 1941-42. The initial erosion of the colonial position occurred in Indochina after June 1940 following the fall of France. From this vantage point the Japanese were poised to strike southwards against the Malay Peninsula and the Netherlands East Indies. Commencing in December 1941, concurrently with the attack on the American fleet and installations at Pearl Harbour, the military onslaught of the armies of Nippon overwhelmed all in its path. By May 1942, with the fall of Corregidor in the Philippines, the Japanese conquest of colonial Southeast Asia was complete and an era had come to an end. The superiority of Europe, which had sustained the authority of colonial government, was exposed as a hollow myth.

Japanese displacement of the colonial orders provided varying opportunities for local élites to assume political, military, and administrative roles and for aspirant nationalist leaders to communicate with popular constituencies. Although the pace of internal political change was strictly controlled to serve the interests of the Japanese war effort, a nominal independence was conferred in Burma and the Philippines in 1943, and in March 1945 within Indochina. The sponsored entities were far from self-governing and enjoyed an artificial autonomy.

The initial Japanese onslaught within Southeast Asia did not reflect accurately its longer-term military prospects. Not many months after the highpoint of Japanese military success it began to be realized that the early battles had not decided the course of the conflict and that the dispossession of the Japanese position in Southeast Asia would be but a matter of time. Among the deposed colonials there existed differing opinions on the question of restoration of rule.

Only one such country was to pass through the storm of hostilities without enduring an intolerable drain on its national resources. That country, the United States, had held some reservations about the return of the French to Indochina and had long committed itself to complete independence for the Philippines. For the Netherlands and France, the Second World War had sapped resources but not the inclination for colonial restoration. They had both experienced the double humiliation of occupation and liberation. Their exiled leaders regarded colonies as compensating assets which would make up for the deprivation exacted by the years of war. They looked forward to returning to Southeast Asia but their plans, which indicated meagre knowledge of the political condition of their colonial possessions, represented vaguely conceived proposals for constitutional change and so provided limited prospects of attracting indigenous support.[2] British proposals for Burma envisaged a stately progress towards self-government, but they were also framed with limited reference to political reality. In the event they were overturned not only by the prospect of violent resistance by local nationalists, but also by the policy pursued by the Supreme Allied Commander for Southeast Asia, Admiral Mountbatten, who accorded early recognition to the undisputed Burmese nationalist leader, Aung San. Proposals for restoration *per se* in Malaya were not challenged locally, although some modification of London's plans for constitutional change became necessary in the face of communal-nationalist reaction. Of all the colonial powers, only the United States was committed to immediate political independence for its Southeast Asian ward.

### The Southeast Asia Command and the Problem of 'Liberation'

At the Quebec Conference in August 1943 an Anglo-American decision was taken to set up a separate Southeast Asia Command (SEAC). Its responsibilities in the war against Japan were confined geographically to those parts of the region bordering on Britain's primary area of interest in Asia, the Indian Ocean. Within its purview lay Burma, Thailand, Malaya, and Sumatra. During the Potsdam Conference in July 1945, however, in the expectation that the war against Japan would last at least another year, the combined chiefs of staff accepted a British proposal to transfer responsibility for the entire Netherlands East Indies and for Indochina south of the sixteenth parallel to the Southeast Asia Command. This meant that, with the exception of what is now North Vietnam and a slice of South Vietnam, together with most of Laos and the Philippines, the entire area of Southeast Asia became the responsibility of Admiral Mountbatten. The transfer of responsibility, which occurred concurrently with the unanticipated early surrender of Japan, had far-reaching political consequences.

At the moment of the assumption of additional responsibility by SEAC the resources at its disposal were quite inadequate for its assigned task.[3] It was deficient equally in political intelligence of the consequences of colonial defeat and Japanese domination. In the Netherlands East Indies and in Indochina significant delays occurred from the day of Japanese surrender until the establishment of an effective SEAC presence. This period of interregnum produced a political vacuum which was filled by nationalist groups who obtained arms and some assistance from the Japanese. In Indochina responsibility for occupation north of the sixteenth parallel was in the charge of the Chinese under Generalissimo Chiang Kai-shek, who proved obstructive towards French goals until February 1946 when France renounced extra-territorial rights in China, in addition to making other concessions. The returning Dutch and French were both faced with political *faits accomplis* which they sought to overcome through *force majeure*. Britain was to meet local resistance only in Burma, where a successful military campaign had been come through *force majeure*. Britain was to meet local resistance from the Burmese force who had been trained by them, but who were, nevertheless, prepared to take up arms to prevent a colonial restoration.

The end of 1945 saw, therefore, an incomplete and contested restoration in the Netherlands East Indies, Indochina, and Burma and a commitment to an early transfer of sovereignty in the Philippines. This situation held out the prospect of a transformation in the international condition of Southeast Asia.

## The Struggle for Independence

The first country to obtain independence was the Philippines in July 1946. The last to do so was Singapore which seceded from Malaysia in August 1965. In historical perspective, twenty-one years represent an exeedingly short space of time. Nonetheless, in considering the foreign relations of the states which emerged during that period it is necessary to examine the stages of international political change and not just the broad compass. The process of independence within Southeast Asia was a mixed activity involving widely differing experiences. There were both compliant and dogged colonials and the manner of attainment of independence had a direct bearing on national attitudes to foreign policy. In one special case, however, the end of the Pacific War did not see an attempt to obstruct restoration by the colonial power, but, instead, a determination to preserve a long-standing independence. Thailand had been the only state within Southeast Asia to survive the territorial acquisitiveness of colonialism. It is appropriate to begin this consideration of the emergence of new states with an analysis of the international position of Thailand following the surrender of Japan.

## Thailand: Political Rehabilitation and a New Alignment

At the cessation of hostilities, Thailand was in an uncertain position. It had been associated closely with Japan from 1941, succumbing to a suzerainty imposed by *force majeure*. In January 1942 the military government of Marshal Phibun had declared war on the side of Japan against the Western Allies. Even before this undertaking, Thailand had enriched itself territorially, with Japanese support, at the expense of the French colonial domain in Laos and Cambodia. Subsequently title was secured to bordering provinces in British Burma and Malaya.[4]

The radical change in Japanese military fortunes did not bring political disaster to Thailand. During the war an element within its political élite made a realistic adjustment to the prospect of American dominance in Asia. Thus, while Britain and France were naturally aggrieved at the war-time record and alignment of Thailand, their American ally adopted a different position. The American government responded sympathetically to Thai political dissent, expressed in a restoration of civilian rule and viewed the country as a victim of unfortunate international circumstances and not as a co-belligerent of Japan.

In the circumstances, Britain and France were obliged to defer to the wishes of their more powerful ally who resisted successfully a demand for Allied reorganization and control of the Thai armed forces on the lines of American policy for Japan. Thailand came to be considered little differently from any other country liberated from enemy tutelage. Its independence was not challenged and its international status was assured. Britain and France had to be satisfied with the return of those provinces detached from their colonial possessions.

Although Thailand enjoyed a reputation for a foreign policy which avoided undue entanglement with any one state, the years leading up to the Pacific War had been marked by a sensitive accommodation to the dominant powers in Asia. With the defeat of Japan and the onset of a debilitating civil war in China, the role of dominant power was assumed by the United States. From this juncture Thai external and also internal policy was governed increasingly by the criterion of securing the approval of Washington. Initially, however, this policy was coupled with opposition to the position of France in Asia and support for national independence movements. For example, the post-war Pridi administration did not object to the establishment of a Viet-Minh mission in Bangkok which engaged in the purchase of arms and supplies as well as in propagandizing for its cause. In September 1947 several ministers expressed their support for a Southeast Asian League; a short-lived regional front organization against colonialism sponsored by the Viet-Minh.[5]

Thailand's post-war relationship with the United States was of special importance in that it underpinned the domestic position of civilian politicians who utilized external approval to fend off the political ambitions of a discredited military. However, by the end of 1947 the military reasserted themselves, assisted by civilian political dissension and the repercussions of the untimely death of young King Ananda in June 1946. By April 1948 changing criteria for Western approval made it possible for the wartime premier, Marshal Phibun, to return to office and dispense with the democratic window-dressing provided by civilian ministers. In an inaugural speech, Phibun appealed to the Western powers on the basis of his government's anti-Communist posture and the prospect of an emerging threat from the Chinese mainland. American recognition of the extra-constitutional transfer of power to the military regime was speedily forthcoming. The Cold War had come to dominate the American outlook. The orientation and stability of the new Thai government was a great attraction for Washington and compensated for any reserve held about the manner of its taking office. British interests also coincided with those of the Thai government to erase any sense of grievance harboured over the post-war settlement after the Malayan Communist party had launched an insurrection in June 1948 and a state of emergency was declared throughout the adjacent peninsula.

The Phibun government demonstrated a measure of caution, nonetheless, before entering into an unequivocal alignment with the United States. Its inclination was clear, but it was careful to wait upon events before making a decisive commitment. Thus, during 1949 tolerance was shown still to the activities of the Viet-Minh in Bangkok. It has been argued that it was thought 'unwise to antagonize the Viet-Minh, at least until it was known that the United States and Britain were prepared to support the French' in the war in Indochina.[6] In the absence of American encouragement, there was only tepid response in Bangkok to the Philippine initiative in 1949 for a Pacific (anti-Communist) pact. The Thai government awaited American involvement, which came only after Communist success in China. That involvement manifested itself in diplomatic recognition of the French-sponsored states in Indochina, in particular the government of Bao Dai in Vietnam. At the end of February 1950 Thailand followed suit with recognition. Phibun then reversed the indulgent attitude to the Viet-Minh, whose representatives ceased to be welcome in Bangkok. The full extent of the Thai alignment became evident in July 1950 when 4,000 ground troops were sent to fight in Korea as part of the UN force. This gesture sealed the growing bond between Thailand and the United States which was to be sustained over the next two decades, despite periodic soul-searching and reservations about the perils of rigid association. Subsequent regimes continued Thailand's pro-Western and anti-Communist orientation, in part because it satisfied the needs of external security, and also because such association, involving the approval and material benefaction of the dominant power in Asia, facilitated the primacy of the military in politics.

### The Philippines: A Foreign Policy of Dependence

The Philippines was the first new state of Southeast Asia to acquire independence. Consolidated in territorial form by Spain, the Philippines experienced a controlled and peaceful progress towards self-government under the tutelage of its second colonial master. Full independence had been promised in 1934 when the American Congress approved the Tydings-McDuffie Act which provided for an interim period of shared rule prior to the transfer of sovereignty in 1946. The Japanese invasion and occupation was not permitted to stand in the way of this timetable for independence.

During the course of the occupation, armed resistance had been conducted against the Japanese by a peasant-based organization, the *Hukbalahap* (People's Anti-Japanese Army) which had a Communist leadership. This organization represented not only resistance to the Japanese, but also a challenge to a social and economic élite who, in the main, had co-operated with the occupying power.[7] The American Supreme Commander, General Douglas McArthur, was to overlook the matter of collaboration during the occupation and did not place obstacles to political participation in the path of those men who had been associated with the Japanese-inspired independence of October 1943. Instead, he indicated his personal support in the elections of April 1946 for an active collaborator, Manuel Roxas, instead of for President Osmēna, who had spent the war years in Washington. In the event, Roxas became the first elected president of an independent Philippines, whose political heights were commanded by a traditional ruling class indebted to a United States government which regarded the Philippines as a critical component in the Asian power balance.

A dependent economic relationship between the Philippines and the United States was established in advance of the formal transfer of power, as the task of post-war reconstruction was too immense to be postponed. An American Congressional Trade Act provided a preferential position for goods and raw materials entering the United States market for a limited period and a Rehabilitation Bill provided economic assistance and financial compensation for war-damage and war-service. American bounty was combined with conditions, however, and provoked resentment which was to become progressively more strident over the decades which spanned the relationship. For example, major repayments under the Rehabilitation Bill were made dependent on approval of the Trade Act, which included the provocative provision that American citizens would enjoy equal rights with Filipinos to exploit the country's natural resources and to operate its public utilities. This 'parity' provision, was to be of limited practical significance, but assumed a symbolic notoriety to wound Filipino national pride. It represented a rude awakening to nationhood on the part of a people who had expected better of the guardian-power to whom they had demonstrated their loyalty. In the light of economic circumstances, however, and the stark reality of an unequal relationship there was little alternative but to accede to the conditions for American benefaction.[8]

A sense of gratitude and the force of expediency promoted a subordinate relationship in the penumbra of the United States. At the moment of independence, the fact of a shattered economy and the memory of a speedy and fearsome Japanese occupation pointed up a condition of extreme vulnerability and so shaped the country's international orientation. At the same time, rural unrest in Central Luzon underlined the coincidence of ideological interest between the government of the new state and its American protector. In March 1947, the government of the Philippines made available sites for American military bases on ninety-nine year leases. This arrangement was followed by a military assistance agreement between the two countries.

The Philippines attained independence with the active sponsorship of the colonial power and the advent of the first new Southeast Asian state made little impact within the region. This was not solely because nationalists elsewhere, in Indonesia for example, were unduly preoccupied with their own problems and priorities. More importantly, the nature of the association with the United States constrained any inclination to demonstrate nationalist spirit and shrouded the identity of the Republic. In consequence, the Philippines acquired a reputation for being a spokesman for American interests. For example, at the historic Asian Relations Conference held in New Delhi in March 1947 Filipino representatives applauded the record of the United States to the consternation of other delegates. An expression of interest in the political welfare of fellow-Asians failed to modify the stereotype of the Philippines as a dutiful client of the United States.

Domestic and external challenge consolidated the relationship with the United States. At the end of 1949, following a flagrantly corrupt presidential election, the Communist-led Huks resolved their long-standing internal differences and decided on armed struggle to achieve their ideological goals. The high point of this uprising occurred during 1950; as a result American military aid and advice was made available and contributed to the success of counter-insurgency operation. In January 1950 the American Secretary of State, Dean Acheson, described the Philippines as a vital link in an off-continental island chain represented as the forward defence perimeter of the United States. The significance of the Philippines to the United States was further enhanced after the outbreak of the Korean War in June. In August the first of a five-battalion combat team — financed by the United States — was despatched to Korea to fight under United Nations command. The military relationship was placed on a more formal footing with the American attempt to bolster the position of Japan in Asia as a counter to a communist China. To compensate the Philippines for its willingness to adhere to the Japanese Peace Treaty, the United States committed itself in August 1951 to a treaty of mutual security pledging assistance in the event of armed attack.

Although the Mutual Security Pact of 1951 did not match the formal content of the NATO accord, it represented a commitment of sufficient substance to strengthen the special relationship, despite some signs of an incipient neutralism within a boisterous Congress. The relationship did not involve onerous obligations detrimental to Filipino interests and, if the Philippines did not shine as a beacon of Asian nationalism, it received economic bounty to compensate for a subordinate status. For example, in November 1950 a substantial allocation of economic assistance was tied to a reorganization of the economy and a revision of fiscal policy recommended by an American survey mission. The reality of Philippine foreign policy at this early juncture was a special relationship and a special dependence, both economic and military.

### Burma: A Non-Offensive Foreign Policy

Britain, like the United States, was to prove a compliant colonial power in the face of a less tractable situation than that in the Philippines. Before the war Burma had been provided with some of the attributes of internal self-government, but little serious thought had been given to the question of a target date for independence proper. In April 1943, however, the British wartime coalition cabinet enunciated a new policy for Burma which was to promote complete self-government within the British Commonwealth 'as soon as circumstances permitted'.

Burma lay within the military orbit of the Southeast Asia Command; and the views of Admiral Mountbatten on the question of political restoration served the interests of youthful nationalists within the Japanese-sponsored Burma National Army. He saw little point in denying their political participation if in the process the British antagonized the organization to whom power would most probably have to be transferred.[9] Mountbatten's attitude was determined also by the need to ensure the success of military operations against the Japanese, but he was mindful of the value of stable government in the wake of military success. He therefore acquiesced in the proferred co-operation of the Burmese nationalists with the British re-entry into the country.

By the time the civil government had returned from its place of exile in India in October 1945, the nationalists organized politically within the Anti-Fascist People's Freedom League had a firm place in popular affections and were able to dictate the pace of the transfer of power. The Burmese nationalists, led by Aung San, were radically different in outlook from the accommodating political élite of the Philippines. They saw themselves as combating a colonial system which had pauperized the people of Burma through its toleration of

alien economic control. Uncomprising in attitude and well enough
rooted in popular support to risk a test of strength with the civil
administration, they were unwilling to accept British criteria of
preparedness for independence or the exclusion of ethnic non-
Burman areas from the political orbit of the new state. The British
government, awake to the limitations of its resources and con-
scious of the undesirability of trying to hold Burma by force of arms
were obliged to concede a rescheduling of the timetable for independence. They were obliged also to tolerate Burma's rejection of membership of the Commonwealth.

Initial agreement on a rapid progress to indepence was concluded
in January 1947. A transitional form of government continued
during the remainder of the year despite the murder of Aung San
and his senior colleagues, and by October a final agreement was
reached on independence. This took place on 4 January 1948. With
independence there followed a tempestuous period of internal
challenge not just to national government but also to the idea of a
Union of Burma. Ideology and ethnicity in combination and as
separate forces served as the basis for widespread insurrection which
failed eventually, in large part, because of the same absence of unity
among the disaffected which characterized the country as a whole.
✓ With national integrity subject to challenge foreign relations occupied
a subordinate place. Nonetheless, external associations were established. For example, the final break with Britain had been cordial
and an agreement was made to provide training for the Burmese
armed forces. Also, a lend-lease agreement was negotiated with the
United States. Nationalist China responded to diplomatic overtures
and sponsored Burma's admission into the United Nations in April
1948. Such overtures reflected the smaller country's geopolitical
position rather than any ideological commitment. Even in its early
and precarious phase of existence, Burma through the voice of its
Prime Minister, U Nu, had begun to indicate, if tentatively, a non-
aligned approach to foreign relations.

Non-alignment, however, was not to flourish as a foreign policy for
Burma or any other new state until the early 1950s. For Burma,
✓ internal political challenge was linked to external associations.
Thus, in Moscow, the Union government was portrayed as a puppet
regime, while the successful Communist revolutionaries in China
offered support openly to the insurrectionist Burmese Communist
Party. In these circumstances, there was a move to solicit British
and American assistance to underpin the existence of the precarious
union. The Communists had shown themselves to be violently
antagonistic, but Britain possessed a store of good will through its
compliant attitude to the transfer of power, while the United States

basked still in the anti-imperialist reputation of Roosevelt. In June 1949 U Nu suggested to the Burmese Parliament 'It is now time that we should enter into mutually beneficial treaties, defence and economic, with countries of common interest'.[10] Such an initiative did not meet with a positive response. The United States did not, yet, advocate the containment of Communist China, while the supply of military assistance to Burma was regarded as the obligation of the former colonial power. Britain, for its part, was less than sympathetic to the policy of the Union government on the resolution of internal conflict. The persistence of traditional attitudes to the minority peoples, particularly the Karens, served to strain relations and the outcome was the abrogation by Burma of the post-independence military agreements.

By the end of 1949 Burma was faced with the realization that the Western powers had a limited interest in its security. At the same time the Communist countries sustained their hostile regard. Given the *fait accompli* of a Communist China, the Burmese became obliged to provide for security through a policy of non-offence, which is probably a more accurate description of subsequent Burmese practice in foreign relations than the conventional term 'non-alignment' with which the country became identified. Burma became the first non-Communist state to accord diplomatic recognition to Peking, which was reciprocated within two days. U Nu explained: 'Our tiny nation cannot have the effrontery to quarrel with any power. And least, among these, could Burma afford to quarrel with the new China'. The new China, however, was not to modify its open hostility to the government in Rangoon until, in the aftermath of the Korean war, it transformed its general attitude to Asian neutrals. Burma, undaunted, sought amicable relations where they could be found and in particular strengthened its association with the India of Mr Nehru, who encouraged a conciliatory policy as the most effective way of coping with a resurgent China. But such propensities did not forbid the acceptance of Western economic aid. In September 1950, after the outbreak of the Korean war, the United States responded to a Burmese approach of the previous March and agreed to provide economic assistance.

By the outbreak of the Korean war Burma was groping towards a viable foreign policy. It entertained a modest association with the West, while looking hopefully for some change in Communist outlook which would permit a greater assurance of stability in its external relations.

*Indonesia: Revolution and an Independent Foreign Policy*
Indonesia was the first of the new states of Southeast Asia to declare

its independence. But recognition of this status was not achieved until the end of 1949 because of the determined attempts by the Dutch at colonial restoration.

During the period of the occupation a junction took place between those willing to accommodate themselves to Japanese demands and organization in order to promote nationalist goals, and the governing Japanese military who wished to eradicate Dutch influences and exploit the resources of the Indies to prosecute the war. Preparations for a Japanese-sponsored independence began in the wake of a reversal of military fortunes. In September 1944 the Japanese announced their intention to accord independence. Serious preparations for Indonesian participation did not take place, however, until March 1945, while measures to effect a transfer of power were authorized by the Japanese Supreme Commander in Southeast Asia only a week before his country's capitulation. In the event, the declaration of independence was a product of Indonesian volition and Japanese acquiescence.[11]

On 17 August 1945 nationalist leaders, Sukarno and Hatta, proclaimed the independence of Indonesia as a sovereign unitary state with jurisdiction over the former territory of the Netherlands East Indies. The Dutch response was to dismiss the declaration as of little consequence and as the action of Japanese puppets. The British government had entered into a civil affairs agreement with the Dutch to enable a reversion to colonial authority as soon as the task of SEAC was completed in the Indies. But on arrival in Java, the under-strength and under-equipped SEAC forces found functioning an administration of a recognizable kind. This administration which enjoyed local support and access to Japanese arms was in a position to obstruct the primary function of SEAC, namely disarmament and repatriation of Japanese servicemen and the liberation and protection of military and civilian internees, many of whom were in camps in the interior of Java. The shortage of resources and the presence of the Republican Administration obliged the senior SEAC officer, Lieutenant-General Christison, to tolerate the embryo government where it exercized control in order to fulfil his principal obligations. Van Mook, the Dutch Lieutenant-Governor, was to argue that this precipitate step irrevocably prejudiced the future and 'gave the republic a quasi-international status'.[12]

Admiral Mountbatten had advocated discussions between the Dutch and the nationalists at the outset as a matter of military expediency. Van Mook was willing to negotiate but was repudiated by his government, which was determined not to concede any form of recognition to a regime which Dutch military commanders argued could be dislodged with a whiff of grapeshot. However, ferocious resistance by Indonesian irregulars, especially against British forces in the Javanese port of Surabaya in November 1945, plus pressure from SEAC, convinced the Dutch government that there was no course other than negotiations if they wished to begin a restoration in the Indies.

By March 1946, with the beginning of negotiations and following a progressive return of Dutch troops to Java and the outer islands, the Republican leadership became aware of the futility of denying the reality of partial Dutch restoration and recognized that claims at variance with the facts would not advance their cause. Accordingly, the Republican Prime Minister and principal negotiator, Sutan Sjahrir, sought to secure recognition of de facto authority in Java and Sumatra as a first step towards ultimate independence. At Linggadjati, in November 1946 Republican and Dutch representatives agreed in principle on a federal structure for Indonesia within which the Republic would have a prominent place. Indeed, it was the fact of a Republic exercizing authority within part of the Indies that prompted the Dutch to propose a federal solution.[13] In the agreement, the Dutch recognized the de facto authority of the Republic in Java, Madura, and Sumatra, but refused to acknowledge it as a separate international entity apart from the projected United States of Indonesia. This accord affected the recognition policy of other states. Thus, whereas the United States, Britain, and Australia, among others, recognized the de facto status of the Republic, the Dutch were deemed still to be the de jure power — even by the Soviet Union who had first raised the matter of Indonesia before the United Nations.

The Linggadjati Agreement was accepted by the Dutch and Republican governments in March 1947, but the accord concealed conflicting interpretations of the place of the Republic within the projected federal order. By this stage the Nationalists had come to enjoy growing international attention as their determined resistance attracted the mass media. Asian support for their cause was also speedily forthcoming — initially from the interim government of India, which requested that Britain withdraw Indian troops serving with SEAC in Java. Muslim ties were utilized to engender sympathy in the Middle East, while the Labor government in Australia became a cautious advocate of the Republican cause.

By July 1947 a position of deadlock had been reached on the interpretation of the Linggadjati Agreement, especially the provision concerning the status of the Republic within the federal arrangement. Dutch attempts to resolve the problem through *force majeure* in July 1947 (and again in December 1948) and the promotion of additional constituent states in territory seized from the nationalists undermined the physical existence of the Republic. Between the first and second Dutch 'police actions', a United Nations 'Good Offices Committee' succeeded in promoting an agreement (in January 1948) which, although much less favourable to the Republic than that of Linggadjati, postponed a renewal of Dutch military intervention. When it became evident in December 1948 that the objective of the Dutch was to liquidate the Republic, effective international pressures were placed on Holland to withdraw — especially by the United States government. In addition, the Dutch were compelled to reconsider their policy in the face of determined guerilla action by Republican forces. In April 1949 negotiations began again and led to a conference at The Hague where a formal transfer of sovereignty from Holland took place in December 1949. The Hague Conference provided for a federal United States of Indonesia, but during the following year a unitary state replaced the federal structure.

Independence for Indonesia did not result in a total transfer of the territory of the Netherlands East Indies. The Dutch, who sought to retain a foothold partly in the expectation of the disintegration of the culturally diverse new state, refused to permit the incorporation of the western half of the island of New Guinea. At the Round Table Conference at The Hague, which arranged the transfer of power, it was agreed to set aside the question of West New Guinea for further discussion to begin within a year. This matter was not speedily resolved, but bedevilled the post-colonial relationship during the rest of the decade.[14]

At the outset of independence, the experiences of the revolutionary period prompted a deep concern with internal political integration and an abiding suspicion that external forces might be tempted to promote the fragmentation of Indonesia. Apart from legend, there was no historical precedent for the effective territorial unity of the new state before the Dutch had consolidated their colonial domain. Indeed, the uneven pattern and establishment of administrative control, together with a protracted religious and cultural infusion had not promoted any great unifying tradition. It was this diversity which the returning Dutch had sought to exploit in order to undermine the Republic proclaimed in August 1945.

With independence there was full awareness of the bi-polar distribution of world power and a concurrent desire to retain complete independence of action in this context. The experience of the revolution was relevant to this attitude. The United States had been tepid in its backing for Indonesian statehood until the evident failure of the Dutch to enforce a political decision by military means transformed political attitudes in Washington. This experience induced a conviction that the United States had acted primarily as an ally of the Dutch and might well have let the Republic founder had not the quality of nationalist resistance and the force of world opinion made such an impact. This sense of reserve towards the United States revived during the 1950s, and was encouraged by the evident reluctance of the United States to resume the type of pressure on the Dutch which had expedited the transfer of sovereignty and which might also persuade them to relinquish the territory of West New Guinea.

A Communist insurrection at Madiun in September 1948 produced an equal suspicion of the Soviet Union. The uprising was in part an outcome of the hard line associated with the inauguration of Cominform in 1947. The episode occured shortly after the sponsored return from exile in Moscow of the veteran Indonesian Communist leader, Musso. The uprising was essentially an internal affair and did not reflect any projection of Soviet power. But the Soviet government supported the revolt on radio and denounced President Sukarno as a Japanese quisling.

A dread of colonialism, a suspicion of great powers capitalist or Communist, and an acute concern with national integrity marked the initial international orientation of independent Indonesia. Such an orientation was not remarkable given the revolutionary experience of Indonesia and the implications of a bi-polar world. It was expressed in a desire for a *politik bebas-aktif*: literally, a free and active foreign policy which would avoid all entanglements, especially those associated with the Cold War.

*Southeast Asia in June 1950*
By June 1950 independence had been acquired by the Philippines, Burma, and Indonesia, while the international status of Thailand was well assured. The Cold War had already intruded into the region in the form of internal revolts launched by local Communist parties. In Burma, Indonesia, and colonial Malaya these revolts occurred during 1948, while in the Philippines insurrection proper reached its climax in the first half of 1950. In Indochina the Communist-led Viet-Minh had been engaged in violent contest with the French since the end of 1946.

Some have argued that the revolts were the direct consequence of a youth conference, held in Calcutta in February 1948, whose resolutions reflected the militant line of the Cominform. However, it is most unlikely that precise directions for revolution were communicated at Calcutta.[15] The occasion did serve to convey the current outlook of Moscow but its intervention in insurrection in Southeast Asia was essentially propagandistic. It involved the rejection of the independence of the new states and the portrayal of their leaders as puppets of the colonial powers. In one important respect, there was credibility in such a charge. Within Southeast Asia, major foreign exchange-earning undertakings were still controlled by European interests. The transfers of power had not transformed the economic structure of the new states. Even in Indonesia, where the progress to independence had been fraught with bitter conflict, the Dutch had preserved a significant economic stake.

Insurrection in Southeast Asia did not promote common international attitudes on the part of those states subject to the experience. Indeed, with the exception of Burma, which shared a common but undemarcated border with the Chinese People's Republic, the other new states faced with insurrection treated it, in the main, as an internal matter. Much more significant for international relations within Southeast Asia was the establishment of the Chinese People's Republic in October 1949 and the outbreak of war in Korea which drew the United States more directly into the political and military affairs of the region.

The intervention of North Korean forces across the thirty-eighth parallel in June 1950 produced a swift and dramatic American involvement which extended beyond the Korean peninsula to Indochina. A special technical and economic mission of the Economic Co-operation Administration (ECA) was despatched to Saigon in August 1950, while a military advisory assistance group soon followed. The subsequent intervention of Chinese forces in the Korean conflict confirmed for the American government that there existed a close congruence of interests between themselves and the French in Southeast Asia. American commitment was to be demonstrated subsequently in the volume of economic and military aid provided which by the spring of 1954, comprised 78 per cent of the total cost of prosecuting the war in Indochina against the Viet-Minh. American interest was institutionalized, after the military defeat of France, in the Southeast Asia Treaty Organization, which was established to create a barrier against further Communist territorial advance in the region.

Korea marked a turning point in a sense other than the more direct involvement of the United States in Southeast Asian affairs. During the course of the war, and as a consequence of a change in international outlook by the Soviet Union and China, neutralism or non-alignment became a more viable foreign policy. At Colombo in April 1954 Burma and Indonesia combined with other Asian countries to draw attention to the danger of great power intervention in Indochina. The high point of this trend to ameliorate the major global confrontation was the conference of Asian and African countries held at Bandung in Indonesia in April 1955 at which Chinese and Communist Vietnamese enthusiasm for peaceful coexistence met with warm response from a number of Southeast Asian States. Before considering this development, however, it is necessary to take account of the situation in Indochina which preceded it.

## Towards a Transfer of Power in Indochina

### VIETNAM

French attempts at restoration in Indochina were resisted with vigour in Vietnam, where a Communist-led popular movement for independence (the Viet-Minh) filled the political vacuum in the interregnum following the Japanese capitulation. As a fighting force, the Viet-Minh were then merely a small élite group but they profited from the decision of the Potsdam Conference to share the function of dispossessing the Japanese in Indochina between the forces of Generalissimo Chiang Kai-shek and those of SEAC. The principal strength of the Viet-Minh was north of the sixteenth parallel where they had recruited successfully among the hill tribes. The Japanese encouraged the initial seizure of power and made no attempt to stand in the way when a thousand armed members of the Viet-Minh entered Hanoi on 19 August 1945. They provided arms and training and a number of Japanese soldiers fought with the Viet-Minh against the French.[16]

The leadership of the Viet-Minh was aware that it had inherited a situation of interregnum and that it would be necessary to make provision against a French attempt at restoration. For this reason, efforts were made to secure international recognition of independence especially from the United States whose attitude had appeared favourable, if equivocal. The formal declaration of the independence of the Democratic Republic of Vietnam by Ho Chi Minh in Hanoi on 2 September 1945, attended by military representatives of the Western Allies, attempted to identify the Viet-Minh government with the mainstream of democratic liberalism. The Declaration of Independence included the sanguine assertion: 'We are convinced that the Allies who have recognized the principles of equality of peoples at the Conferences of Teheran and San Francisco cannot but recognize the independence of Viet-Nam'.[17] This plea, together with private communications, made no impact either on the Western Powers or on the Soviet Union, which had already come to terms with the regime of Chiang Kai-shek at the expense of the Chinese Communists.

In the absence of international recognition, the Viet-Minh

required time to consolidate their internal position and such time was to be provided by the Chinese nationalist occupation forces who entered the country in September. The Chiang regime regarded the role of its forces north of the sixteenth parallel as a means of securing concessions from the French. And in the months that it took to negotiate these concessions, including the renunciation of extra-territorial rights in China, the Viet-Minh extended and strengthened its organization.

French plans for Indochina did not match the declaration by Ho Chi Minh's provisional government. In March 1945, following the Japanese *coup de force*, the French government produced a formula which stated *inter alia*: 'The Indochinese Federation will comprise, together with France and the other sections of the community, a "French Union" whose foreign interests will be represented by France. Indochina will enjoy, within this Union, its own freedon'.[18] Such vague promises were hardly acceptable to the Viet-Minh, who braced themselves for an inevitable confrontation.

The area to the south of the sixteenth parallel in Indochina was the responsibility of SEAC whose British and Commonwealth forces arrived in Saigon on 13 September 1945 to find a Viet-Minh administration maintaining essential services. After an initial attempt to fulfil their non-political functions, including disarming the Japanese, without involvement in the internal struggle, their actions made it possible for released French internees to resume political control at the expense of the Viet-Minh.[19] By the end of October, a substantial French military presence had been established in and around Saigon. North of the sixteenth parallel, the Kuomintang forces remained until the end of February 1946 by which time an accord had been reached with the French and the Viet-Minh had extended its popular base.

Given the imbalance of forces, by early 1946 the Viet-Minh were prepared to come to terms with the French in order to avoid an unpropitious confrontation. Initial negotiations bore fruit in the form of an agreement of 6 March whereby the return of French forces north of the sixteenth parallel for a period of five years would not be opposed. In return, the French government recognized 'The Republic [sic] of Viet-Nam as a Free State — forming part of the Indochinese Federation and the French Union'.[20] The March 1946 agreement was considered necessary because of the Viet-Minh failure to secure international recognition and the inevitable prospect of a French military presence north of the sixteenth parallel.

With the re-establishment of the French in Hanoi, subsequent negotiations over the international status of the Viet-Minh regime became more chequered. The lack of progress was a product partly of political circumstances within France and also of the determined opposition to the Viet-Minh from the French High Commissioner for Indochina, Admiral d'Argenlieu, who ensured that the March 1946 accord would not apply in Cochinchina. He inspired the declaration of a Republic of Cochinchina on 1 June 1946 and, from this juncture, the prospects of an accommodation decreased rapidly. From June through to September, Ho Chi Minh engaged himself in fruitless negotiations in Fontainebleau which concluded with a meaningless *modus vivendi*. The following November a dispute over the control of customs in the port of Haiphong — the point of entry for arms supply to the Viet-Minh — led to a physical confrontation with the French. A Viet-Minh uprising the next month in Hanoi marked the end of talking and the beginning of fighting, which did not run its violent course until the signature of cease-fire agreements in Geneva in July 1954.

During the course of the military conflict the French, encouraged by the United States, sought to establish a constitutional basis for their position and to attract popular support to counter the nationalist appeal of the Viet-Minh. The unity of Vietnam (including Cochinchina) was conceded and in March 1949 the country was accorded the doubtful rank of an Associated State of the Federation of Indochina within the French Union — a body which resembled the British Commonwealth in form, but which reserved to itself full powers in external affairs. Bao Dai, the former Emperor of Annam who had abdicated in favour of the Viet-Minh Provisional Government in August 1945, was appointed head of state. The independence accorded was subject to the limitations imposed through membership of the French Union.

CAMBODIA AND LAOS

The two lesser states of Indochina proceeded to independence as a consequence of the course of conflict in Vietnam. Nationalist activity had been of minimal significance in these protectorates and the writ of the Indochinese Communist party, based in the main on the ethnic Vietnamese, did not extend there in any effective sense until after the Second World War.

In the case of Cambodia, the movement towards independence occurred gradually and without major struggle. The French conceded formal autonomy by 1949 although the substance of sovereignty remained in their hands. Internal political reaction to this façade of independence alerted the young monarch, Norodom Sihanouk, to the Viet-Minh and non-Communist nationalist challenge to his position. He was prompted to demand a complete independence and during 1953 set out on a diplomatic circumambulation, passing through Western capitals, to plead his country's case. By the middle of that year French obduracy was eroded under the pressure of military events in Vietnam and in Laos and an increasing loss of political will in Paris. A further series of agreements was then concluded which the Cambodian king was able to represent as the acquisition of complete independence. As a consequence, he returned from a self-imposed exile in the western provinces of Cambodia to celebrate the attainment of independence in Phnom Penh on 9 November 1953. International recognition of this status was to be accorded following the Geneva Conference of 1954.

In Laos the French restoration to the royal capital of Luang Prabang was delayed until May 1946, in part because of the need to come to terms with the occupying Chinese forces of Chiang Kai-shek. The French return saw the enforced exile in Thailand of a short-lived independence movement (Lao Issara), led by members of the cadet branch of the royal family, as well as the crushing of an associated resistance group inspired by the Viet-Minh and based in the main on Vietnamese living in Laos. From this juncture, a process of political development ensued similar to that which transpired in Cambodia. In August 1946 a *modus vivendi* was concluded, whereby France extended the territorial authority of Luang Prabang and recognized the unity of Laos. In May 1947 the country became a constitutional monarchy within the French Union: a relationship formalized in July 1949, following which the Lao Issara leaders returned to Vientiane. Military and political exigency led in October 1953 to a Treaty of Friendship and Association with France and a reaffirmation of membership in the French Union. But, like Cambodia, Laos was not to receive full international recognition until the conclusion of the Geneva Conference on Indochina in July 1954.

### The Geneva Conference and the Indochinese States

The joint decision to convene an international conference on Indochina and Korea was taken in February 1954 during the course of four power talks on Berlin. The sessions on Indochina did not commence until 8 May. This proved to be an unhappy coincidence for the French in particular and the Western powers in general. The previous day, the Viet-Minh forces had overcome the French military position at Dien Bien Phu. The siege of this fortress had been an agonizing experience and during its course the American government had seriously contemplated military intervention to retrieve the situation. The surrender of Dien Bien Phu was a great psychological blow for the French and also did not assist the negotiating position of the Western Allies, whose unity was subject to strain.

The participants in the Indochina Conference were France, Britain, the United States, the Chinese People's Republic, the Soviet Union, and the three Associated States. In addition, the Viet-Minh were represented by delegates from the Democratic Republic of Vietnam (DRV).[21]

## VIETNAM

Although the State of Vietnam was represented at Geneva, the status of its delegation was not clear. For example, it was pointedly excluded from the Franco-Viet-Minh military commission which arranged the terms of a cease-fire and did not play a part in nego- tiating the line of 'provisional' demarcation along the seventeenth parallel which subsequently was to take on the character of a political boundary. By contrast, the representatives of the Democratic Republic of Vietnam played a prominent role and its Deputy Defence Minister signed the cease-fire agreement with a French counterpart.

Under the terms of the Cease-fire Agreement and the Final Declaration of the Conference, the agreed line of provisional demarcation was to endure until July 1956, when country-wide elections would serve as a preliminary to national unification. The Declaration was not a signed treaty but a statement to which the delegates responded orally and not necessarily with positive consent. The government of the State of Vietnam, headed by the returned exile, Ngo Dinh Diem, rejected its terms and any obligations assumed by France.

From the end of the Conference, Diem acted with resolution to consolidate his position south of the seventeenth parallel against dissident military and disaffected politico-religious sects. By May 1955 he had obtained the unequivocal backing of the American government, which had reserved its position on the agreements reached at Geneva. In August 1954 it had begun to provide economic assistance directly to the Indochinese states and not through France, while in September the United States was the principal sponsor of SEATO which offered protection from aggression to 'the States of Cambodia and Laos and the free territory under the jurisdiction of the State of Vietnam'. Within two years the political consolidation achieved by the Diem government was relatively substantial. In October 1955 Bao Dai was deposed as head of state through a managed referendum and the State of Vietnam gave way in nomen- clature to the Republic of Vietnam, of which Ngo Dinh Diem became president. This Republic secured diplomatic recognition from the allies and associates of the United States, but enjoyed only limited relationships within Southeast Asia.

The northern counterpart of the Republic of Vietnam with its seat of government in Hanoi was linked diplomatically with the Communist international system. Its closest ties then were with the Chinese People's Republic, which had provided training facilities and military assistance for the Viet-Minh forces, and also the Soviet Union. The Geneva settlement gave the DRV much less territorially than had been reflected in its military position in July 1954. During the course of the conference, its Chinese and Soviet allies had persuaded the Vietnamese Communists of the desirability of provisional partition. The weight of these joint pressures and the prospect of American military intervention encouraged a compromise solution. Nonetheless the settlement provided the Viet-Minh regime with its first real opportunity to function as a conventional government. In July 1955 it attempted to begin negotiations to secure the full implementation of the Final Declaration. However, this approach was rejected by Diem with American backing. The ultimate consequence was the support of Hanoi for a southern-based insurgency which began as a rebellion against the Diem government and which reached a critical stage by the end of the decade.[22]

CAMBODIA AND LAOS

Although military conflict in Indochina had centred on control of Vietnam, agreement on Cambodia and Laos proved a greater obstacle to successful accord at Geneva. A major point of dispute was over the demand by the DRV delegate that Communist-sponsored resistance movements in those two countries should be recognized with representatives at the conference table. In the event, the Geneva Conference agreed to treat Cambodia and Laos on a different basis from Vietnam.

In the case of Cambodia, an accord was reached whereby its territorial integrity under one government was recognized, together with a pledge by the Viet-Minh to withdraw their forces. Cambodia achieved notable diplomatic success by securing general acceptance of its right not to be bound by any imposed neutralization and by being the only non-Communist state of Indochina to have its own military commander sign a cease-fire agreement with the DRV plenipotentiary.

During the latter stages of the Indochina war, the Cambodian government had sought military protection from the United States. With its conclusion, there was a real prospect that Cambodia would seek alignment with and security from Washington. However, the speedy withdrawal by the Viet-Minh, the gratuitous commitment from SEATO and a realization that there was little point in provoking the Communists in either China or Vietnam—from whom Cambodia was shielded territorially by the de facto State of Vietnam—in advance of the appearance of any aggressive intent contributed to a reappraisal of foreign policy in the direction of non-alignment.

Although the government of Laos successfully resisted demands at Geneva for the seating of a delegate from the so-called Lao Resistance government, it was unable to ensure the integrity of the country in the same manner as Cambodia. The resistance government was, in effect, the political arm of the Pathet Lao, a Communist sponsored organization formed in August 1950. During the latter stages of the First Indochina War, the Viet-Minh had invaded Laos and had consolidated the position of the Pathet Lao in two provinces close to the Vietnamese border. Because of this position of special advantage, the Pathet Lao were able to avoid being demobilized like their Cambodian equivalents, but were permitted to regroup in the provinces of Phong Saly and Sam Neua pending a political settlement, which meant, in effect, the attainment of independence without political unity.

Laos, therefore, was in a very different position to Cambodia. First of all, internal political divisions were reflected in the absence of territorial unification. In addition, Laos bordered the DRV (North Vietnam), which meant that the Pathet Lao had direct access to external support and asylum, which it was to utilize subsequently. Following Geneva, Prime Minister Souvanna Phouma — a half brother of the nominal leader of the Pathet Lao, Prince Souphanouvong — sought to promote internal political unity through a policy of conciliation and to avoid external intervention by eschewing any foreign commitments.

The negotiations held in Geneva which were concluded in July 1954 marked the second significant stage in the process of independence in Southeast Asia. In effect, four new states emerged as a consequence of that conference, although the international status of two, i.e. both Vietnams, has never been clearly established. Of colonial Southeast Asia, only the British possessions in Malaya, Singapore, and North Borneo remained (plus Portuguese Timor), and by 1955 the development of self-government in the two former territories indicated that colonial status had a limited future. The colonial order which had characterized the region before the Pacific War had been swept aside in the Japanese advance and had never been reconstituted anew. In its place had emerged a number of diverse states with a mixed experience of attaining independence. These states were engaged in feeling their separate ways in an environment that was their own, because it was Southeast Asian, but was, at the same time, also strange and novel because it was part of a wider international system.

References

1 G. J. Resink, *Indonesia's History Between the Myths: Essays in Legal History and Historical Theory*, The Hague, 1968, p. 136.

2 See 'The Declaration of the French Government on Indochina', 23 March 1945 and 'Queen Wilhelmina's Proposal for a Netherlands Commonwealth', 2 December 1942 reprinted in Harold R. Isaacs (*ed.*), *New Cycle in Asia*, New York, 1947, pp. 159–61 and pp. 178–81.

3 See *Post Surrender Tasks*, Section E of the Report to the Combined Chiefs of Staff by the Supreme Allied Commander Southeast Asia 1943–1945, London, H.M.S.O., 1969, p. 282.

4 For an account of Thai–Japanese relations before and after the outbreak of hostilities see Sir Josiah Crosby, *Siam: The Crossroads*, London, 1945.

5 For a first hand account of the origins of the Southeast Asian League see John Coast, *Recruit to Revolution*, London, 1952, p. 52.

6 Donald E. Nuechterlein, *Thailand and the Struggle for Southeast Asia*, Ithaca, 1965, p. 105.

7 The late F. C. Jones has pointed out that the Japanese secured élite co-operation, in part, because of an 'élite fear of peasant radicalism'; *Japan's New Order in Asia*, London, 1954, p. 358; see also David J. Steinberg, *Philippine Collaboration During the Second World War*, Ann Arbor, 1967.

8 For a thoughtful discussion of the unequal relationship see David Wurfel, 'Problems of Decolonization' in Frank H. Golay (ed.), *The United States and the Philippines*, New Jersey, 1966.

9 F. S. V. Donnison, *British Military Administration in the Far East 1943–1946*, London, 1946, p. 337.

10 Quoted in Richard Butwell, *U Nu of Burma*, Stanford, 1963, p. 172.

11 Benedict R. O'G. Anderson, *Java in a Time of Revolution*, Ithaca, 1972, Ch. 4.

12 H. J. Van Mook, *The Stakes of Democracy in South-East Asia*, London, 1950, p. 246. For the best general account of the process of independence see G. McT. Kahin, *Nationalism and Revolution in Indonesia*, Ithaca, 1952. See also Anderson, *op. cit.*

13 A. A. Schiller, *The Formation of Federal Indonesia*, The Hague, 1955, p. 19.

14 Robert C. Bone, *The Dynamics of the Western New Guinea (Irian Barat) Problem*, Ithaca, 1958.

15 Ruth T. McVey, 'The Southeast Asian Revolts' in Cyril E. Black and Thomas P. Thornton (eds), *Communism and Revolution: The Strategic Uses of Political Violence*, New Jersey, 1969.

16 John T. McAlister, *Viet Nam: The Origins of Revolution*, New York, 1969, pp. 215–6.

17 Reprinted in Isaacs, *op. cit.*, p. 165.

18 *Ibid.*, p. 159.

19 McAlister, *op. cit.*, p. 200. See also George Rosie, *The British in Vietnam*, London, 1970.

20 Isaacs, *op cit.*, p. 169.

21 The most complete and exhaustive account of the Geneva Conference is contained in Robert F. Randle, *Geneva 1954: The Settlement of the Indochinese War*, New Jersey, 1969. See also Donald Lancaster, *The Emancipation of French Indochina*, London, 1961; and Philippe Devillers and Jean Lacouture, *End of a War — Indochina, 1954*, London, 1969.

22 An excellent account of the origins of what is known now as the Second Indochina War is provided by Jeffrey Race in *Asian Survey*, May 1970. See also *The Pentagon Papers*, New York, 1971, pp. 67–78.

*Chapter Two*

# FIRST STEPS IN FOREIGN POLICY

By the mid-1950s the foreign policies of the new states had assumed distinctive form. Uniformity, however, was not their characteristic. International outlook was marked by a dualism which reflected the ways in which security was perceived and sought. Apart from the Democratic Republic of Vietnam, linked to the Communist international system, the states of Southeast Asia were either members of the alliance network sponsored by the United States or associated loosely as adherents of a foreign policy of non-alignment.

Non-alignment or neutralism[1] as a policy linking ex-colonial states and portending to lessen international tensions between cold war competitors had been given a practical cast by India's conduct during the latter part of the Korean War. At the climax of the conflict in Indochina, in the spring of 1954, neutral states in Asia found common cause and a vehicle through which to voice their hopes and apprehensions. Burma and Indonesia from Southeast Asia joined with India, Ceylon, and Pakistan at Colombo in April 1954 to call a halt to the war. Their demands were related not only to the independence of the Associated States, but also to the mobilization of opinion against the United States, which was perceived as the potential interventionist power seeking to stem the tide of Asian nationalism. After the settlement in Indochina, Cambodia also was soon to adopt the neutral approach to security in company with Burma and Indonesia and, initially, Laos.

The committed anti-Communist Southeast Asians were Thailand, the Philippines, and South Vietnam. The two former countries were both members of SEATO. Its inaugural conference was held in Manila and the headquarters of the alliance was sited in Bangkok. The political orientation of governing élites in both Thailand and

28

the Philippines was conservative and anti-Communist and if the United States was the natural patron of the Philippines it was also the natural ally of Thailand. The actual importance of these two countries in the arrangements for collective defence was limited. Their contribution was more symbolic than of substance.

Outside the formal structure of SEATO were Cambodia, Laos, and South Vietnam; three successor states offered a gratuitous protection. Of these countries, Cambodia was to reject this offer. Laos began its independent existence with a propensity to non-alignment, but it was not sustained by the late 1950s. The southern portion of Vietnam became closely aligned with the United States. The association developed, however, on a bilateral basis outside of the formal context of SEATO.

## The Foreign Policies of the Neutrals

### BURMA

The foreign relations of Burma developed in an unspectacular manner. A full awareness of its position as a small vulnerable state with serious problems of political order encouraged adherence to a policy of non-alignment which in its non-offensive practice would assist independent existence. Internal dissension had prevented an association with the Commonwealth, which meant that strong political ties with the Western powers could not be expected unless a major threat to the integrity of the Burmese state presented itself. At the same time, any prospects of firm links with the Communist world, arising out of Burmese conceptions of Marxism, were denied at the outset by the negative attitude of the Soviet Union and of the Chinese People's Republic. Given the internal condition of Burma immediately following independence, deep anxiety existed lest the Cold War find domestic expression and facilitate outside intervention. As a consequence, Burma sought a position independent of bloc alignments. Economic and even military assistance was welcomed from any source, provided that in the process there was no infringement of the country's sovereign position. However, a policy of firm adherence to the defence of independence was combined, where necessary, with an expedient accommodation to safeguard that independence. Nowhere was this dualism more apparent than in relations with the Chinese People's Republic with whom Burma shared a common border.

In December 1949 Burma became the first non-Communist country to accord diplomatic recognition to Peking and it then persevered with its efforts to exchange ambassadors in spite of Chinese encouragement for the insurrectionist Burmese Communist party.

Although Burma sought to demonstrate its declared willingness to be friendly with all foreign countries, China was treated with special regard as long as it did not demonstrate marked hostility to the Union government in deeds as well as in words.

The foreign policy of Burma evolved as a unilateral practice which relied upon its self-evident meritoriousness and absence of ill intent to produce a respectful response from the aligned countries of the world. Initially its formal links tended to be closer to the Western powers. In September 1950 an aid agreement was signed with the United States. In June, prior to the agreement, Burma had voted for the Security Council resolution calling on UN members to assist in repelling the invasion across the thirty-eighth parallel in Korea, although it did not make any material contribution to the UN force.

Throughout the Korean episode, the Burmese position was far from consistent with that of the United States. While Burma might afford the luxury of joining in the condemnation of an ally of the Soviet Union, it was obliged to reassess its position with the entry into the war of the Chinese People's Republic. Thus, in February 1951, Burma, in company with India, voted against the American-sponsored resolution before the General Assembly, which charged China with aggression in Korea, on the grounds that its passage would obstruct a negotiated peace. Through the remaining period of the Korean conflict, Burma was associated closely with Indian-inspired attempts to ease cold war tensions. By this stage, Burma was conducting a conventional foreign policy by the standards of many of its ex-colonial peers. Internationally, it demonstrated greater self-confidence as internal insurrections assumed more of a nuisance value and ceased to be a major threat to the integrity of the state.

March 1953 saw the first major Burmese initiative to forestall a dispute which might have assumed dangerous proportions. In that month, the Burmese government requested that the American aid programme be terminated by the end of June. There had been dissatisfaction in Rangoon with the administration of the programme and sharp reaction to the transfer of its direction from the Technical Co-operation Administration to the Mutual Security Administration which suggested the service of Cold War needs. Concurrently, there had been less pressing need for external economic assistance. The ill wind of the Korean War had brought positive benefits to Burma as a consequence of the increase in demand for raw materials. In such circumstances, a foreign aid relationship which appeared to be making limited contribution to national economic development, and which was capable also of provoking internal dissension, could be broken with little economic loss and some political profit. Such explanation, however, serves only to point to contributory factors in the Burmese decision. The concurrent and dominating reason for the initiative which overshadowed the merits and demerits of the aid relationship was the unnerving presence in the northeast of Burma of Kuomintang forces armed and supplied from the Nationalist Chinese-controlled island of Formosa.

The Kuomintang forces, estimated at 10,000 strong, had crossed into Burma in the closing stages of civil war in China and for several years had been partially concealed in the penumbra of insurrection. By 1952, with the force of insurrection spent, the Kuomintang forces, supplied with new American equipment through Formosa, became a more conspicuous warlord presence. The Burmese government was not only resentful of this denial of central authority, but also was alarmed lest the Chinese People's Republic would feel obliged to strike across the border with Burma to safeguard its own security. The primary purpose of the Burmese government in publicizing the issue, which it did by bringing the matter to the attention of the United Nations, was to demonstrate good faith and peaceful intent to the Government in Peking. By rejecting American economic assistance it was to make clear also that it was in no way culpable in the affair.[2]

The Burmese initiative in placing the issue before the United Nations did not produce conclusive results. And it was only in 1961 that the Burmese Army pushed the remaining Kuomintang elements into Thailand and Laos. Nonetheless, the principal purpose of Burmese policy was achieved in publicizing the issue. The Chinese government in Peking appeared content to regard the matter as essentially of Burmese concern. The period during which the KMT question was raised coincided with the outset of a benign phase of Chinese foreign policy in Asia. China's response to the Burmese initiative confirmed the value of Rangoon's placatory policy. In June 1954 Chou En-lai visited Rangoon and, with U Nu, announced joint adherence to the five principles of peaceful coexistence agreed earlier with the Indian Prime Minister. The following December U Nu visited Peking and on his return declared: 'So long as we do not think or plan evil against them, and so long as we are sincere when we say that they have nothing to fear from our direction, and we do not give them any cause for apprehension by allowing ourselves to be used as bases against them, I am convinced the Chinese will not wish us harm'.[3]

In dealings with the major powers, Burma went out of its way to demonstrate its independent credentials, in spite of a deteriorating economic situation aggravated by a growing factionalism within the ruling AFPFL. However, where the special relationship with China was concerned, much greater flexibility was Burmese practice. This relationship was further consolidated in stages from November 1956 when an agreement in principle was reached on the demarcation of the common border, prompted on the Burmese side by grave concern at active support for the insurgent Burmese Communist party. There was a substantial delay until the signing of a formal accord which took place in January 1960 during the first administration of General Ne Win. Concurrently, there was signed also a Treaty of Friendship and Mutual non-Agression.[4]

With these accords with China, Burma vindicated its neutral foreign policy, exemplified in the exercise of independent judgement, for example, in close ties with Israel and a vocal condemnation of the Soviet Union for its invasion of Hungary. At the global level, Burma practised a modest neutralism and felt free of major constraints because of the benevolent attitudes displayed towards it by the great powers, and because it was not in any way involved in disputes of a Cold War character. Regionally, within Southeast Asia, Burma did not assume a vigorous role, but was consistent in support of anti-colonialism.

After the second and decisive intervention of the military in March 1962 General Ne Win did not make any changes in foreign policy and especially in relation to China. Burma, together with Cambodia, took pains during the Sino-Indian War to avoid giving offence to the one power in Asia that was in a position to threaten its security. This conciliatory attitude was sustained until mid-1967 when overseas Chinese conduct in Rangoon, stimulated by the excesses of the Cultural Revolution, impinged on Burmese political life and precipitated a major if temporary breach in relations. This episode served to demonstrate, however, that if Burma was placatory towards China, it had no intention of being servile where its own interests were concerned.

## INDONESIA

The political orientation of the rulers of newly independent Indonesia was towards internal order and reconstruction. Those in the seat of power wished to put the spirit of revolution to one side and to concentrate on internal development. The disposition of government was towards a modest rather than a strident non-alignment. If there was any disposition in foreign policy it was initially in the direction of the Western world which had been the intellectual mentor for many of the governing élite and which was also the major source of economic assistance and investment capital. Communist countries did not, at first, possess an equivalent appeal.

If foreign policy did not bulk large in governmental priorities, its formation proved, nonetheless, a source of political difficulty. The Indonesian cabinets were coalitions which suffered from a lack of consensus and foreign policy decisions often rebounded into the domestic political arena signalling discord. For example, controversy arose during 1951 over the prospect of Indonesia becoming a party to the Japanese Peace Treaty, and it was argued that signature would be a departure from an independent foreign policy. Much was made of the example of India and Burma, both of whom had refused to send representatives to the San Francisco Conference.

Of greater significance was the domestic crisis which arose from the action of Foreign Minister, Subardjo Djojoadisuryo, who represented Indonesia at San Francisco. While in the United States, Subardjo accepted a $50 million loan under the terms of the United States Mutual Security Act of 1951 which stipulated that any funds allocated should make a full contribution 'to the defence of the free world'. Within Indonesia such a condition was regarded as quite unacceptable and a violation of the country's independent foreign policy. The consequent outcry was so great that the cabinet fell in February 1952.

The succeeding government of Mr Wilopo was also undermined by what was, in effect, a foreign policy issue. This cabinet like its three predecessors had a practical orientation and was concerned to avoid agitational politics. One obstacle to this end was the growing resentment in Indonesia at Dutch obduracy over West Irian which had not been overcome by the diplomatic approaches of Wilopo and his ministers. The popular mood was susceptible to a revival of agitation against the Dutch, whose economic presence was still both ubiquitous and visible. A sense of frustration was in the air, born of the apparent denial of the fruits of an arduous revolutionary struggle. In this climate of growing popular frustration, the government became entangled in an abortive attempt to evict squatters from foreign-owned estates in East Sumatra. The outcome of the episode was a bitter opposition attack on the Wilopo cabinet which contributed to its political demise.

In many respects, the initial experience of Indonesia in foreign relations was less than remarkable. Much the same approach to an independent foreign policy was displayed as that exhibited by other new states. What was especially significant, however, was the extent to which foreign policy issues became closely interconnected with the domestic political process. With the fall of the Wilopo cabinet and its replacement by the more radically-minded government led by Ali Sastroamidjojo, there occurred a perceptible shift in the direction of foreign policy, together with more of a two-way process of interplay between the domestic and international arenas of politics.

Up to the premiership of Ali, the political orientation of Indonesian governments stood in contrast to attitudes prominent during the revolutionary period. With Ali as Prime Minister, a new stridency emerged in harness with a vigorous anti-colonialism. Foreign policy became a much more important aspect of governmental activity coincident with increasing difficulty in domestic policy. Foreign policy aspirations were encouraged by important changes within the international political system. After the death of Stalin and the armistice in Korea, an opening appeared for non-aligned states to play a more active and vocal role. Both the Soviet Union and the Chinese People's Republic had revised their outlook towards the newly independent states and perceived the political advantage in encouraging attitudes which were as much anti-colonial as they were neutral.

The success of Indonesia in establishing its neutral credentials was demonstrated in April 1955 when Bandung served as the venue for a conference of Asian and African countries which, at the time, possessed great emotional and symbolic significance for many of its participants. The conference was convened because the Indonesian Prime Minister was able to secure the support of Mr Nehru for what he conceived as an opportunity for a benevolent India to introduce a benign China to the somewhat suspicious new states of Afro-Asia. The occasion proved to be less consensual than historical myth might suggest.[6] There were aspects of competition between ostensible friends and moments of open discord between advocates of alternative roads to peace and security. Bandung was, nonetheless, a notable achievement for the Indonesian Government which was able to demonstrate that, in spite of domestic difficulties, it presided over a country which enjoyed international standing.

A direct outcome of the Bandung meeting was the development of relations with the Chinese People's Republic. During the course of the conference a dual nationality agreement was negotiated in which China declared itself prepared to renounce jurisdiction over Indonesian-born ethnic Chinese who wished to opt for local nationality. The reversal of a traditional Chinese position reflected the new Chinese outlook in foreign relations.

During the later years of the 1950s the foreign policy of Indonesia paralleled changes that were taking place within the domestic political system. Concurrent with the decline of the parliamentary system foreign policy took on a more radical cast as the campaign to liberate West Irian became more central to Indonesian political life. The failure to secure approval in the United Nations in November 1957 of a favourable resolution on West Irian, followed by a Muslim assassination attempt on Sukarno and the consequent takeover of Dutch assets in Indonesia, reinforced anti-Dutch and anti-American feeling. In addition, regional uprisings beginning in Sumatra in February 1958, linked with external, including Western support, brought into disrepute those political forces within Indonesia which had been most closely identified with Western liberal ideas and practice and whose non-alignment had been modest and unassertive. The failure of the regional revolts and the discrediting of their supporters, internal and external, meant that political radicals in Indonesia reaped the advantage, especially Sukarno whose world view was henceforth to dominate the making of foreign policy. This dominance was reflected in the assertive pursuit of the West Irian campaign in 1960–62 to the point of a diplomatic break with Holland and acceptance of military aid from the Soviet Union. It was demonstrated above all in Sukarno's new ideological formulations, especially the doctrine at the New Emerging Forces (Nefos)[7], through which he attempted to externalize the experience of the Indonesian revolution and to justify international claims not only against the Dutch over West Irian (secured in August 1962), but also against Malaysia.

## CAMBODIA[8]

Following the settlement at Geneva in July 1954 which confirmed the international status of Cambodia, Norodom Sihanouk began to reassess his country's international position. The pressing requirement of an American military guarantee which had been seriously contemplated became less necessary as the Viet-Minh complied with the provisions of the cease-fire agreement. Also, the benevolent regard of China, suggested that an alliance with the United States would be irrelevant and provocative. In addition, Sihanouk was influenced to shift the direction of foreign policy by the example of Nehru's India and by the need to demonstrate to domestic critics that Cambodia's independence was genuine and not a disguised puppet status. By the end of 1954 Sihanouk began to introduce the idiom of neutralism and, following the provision of assurances from both China and North Vietnam at Bandung, Cambodia adopted non-alignment as its foreign policy. The commitment to the declaratory position was so strong that non-alignment was written into the constitution of Cambodia.

Neutrality, as Sihanouk came to describe his country's policy, presumably in order to give it some special distinction, meant in practice a non-committed position in the conflicts of the Cold War and during the second half of the 1950s it was maintained with consistency. Cambodia demonstrated by the scope of its diplomatic contacts and economic links that it was strictly non-aligned. The benign regard of Communist near-neighbours was dependent on non-association with SEATO and the absence of major military ties with the United States. Such self-denial was not to exclude a measure of American military and economic assistance, which was distinguished for Chinese benefit and with Chinese approval from an American military presence. Prince Sihanouk made visits to Communist and non-Communist capitals, while economic assistance was received from both sides in the Cold War. In the case of China, such assistance represented the first grants in aid to a non-Communist country.

Non-alignment for Cambodia involved also abrasive relationships. Independence had removed the French whose intervention since 1863 probably obstructed the absorption of the country by the Thais and Vietnamese. The Geneva settlement had led to the recession of the Viet-Minh threat with a non-Communist portion of Vietnam placed between Cambodia and the Communists. However, traditional antagonisms were to replace ideological ones and Cambodia's post-independence relationship with Thailand and the southern portion of Vietnam was shaped by them. Conflict with these neighbours, which will be discussed in more detail below, came to have a close bearing on Cambodia's relationship with the United States government, which was allied with Thailand in SEATO and committed to the survival of the Diem regime in Saigon. As Cambodia expanded its associations with the Communist world, and in particular with China, with whom diplomatic ties were established in July 1958, relations with Thailand, South Vietnam, and the United States deteriorated; so much so that in the late 1950s agents of all three countries were implicated in plots against the Cambodian state.

Cambodia's foreign policy of non-alignment, like Burma's, had a dual aspect. At one level, it reflected a common unwillingness to become involved in the entanglements of the Cold War; at a different level which was a product of the geopolitics of Cambodia's position, it involved an attempt to match power with countervailing power in the interest of national survival. By exploiting Cold War sensitivities, Prince Sihanouk sought to neutralize any threats to the security of Cambodia. The ability to sustain a prudent balance of self-cancelling forces served as the underlying hallmark of Cambodian foreign policy until the end of the decade. From 1960–61, however, the course of events in Laos and also South Vietnam threw serious doubt on the capability of the United States and its allies to sustain their countervailing role. As a direct consequence, Cambodian non-alignment became transformed into a policy of accomodation to the Communists, initially to the Chinese People's Republic, as Prince Sihanouk concluded that the future of Asia rested in their hands.

## LAOS

After the Geneva Conference on Indochina, the most important problem for those in formal charge of the Laotian state was to secure the integration of the Pathet Lao areas. In order to approach this goal without a revival of international intervention, Prime Minister Souvanna Phouma sought to avoid Cold War entanglements.

At the outset, the government of Laos showed a propensity, towards non-alignment. For example, Prince Souvanna Phouma's successor as Prime Minister in September 1954, Katay Sasorith, although disposed to a close connection with Thailand and antagonistic to the Pathet Lao and their backers, did not align his country in a way that would provoke external Communist intervention. In March 1956 Souvanna Phouma, once again Prime Minister, revived attempts to resolve the outstanding problem of political integration which was obstructed by the determination of the Pathet Lao to consolidate their political base in the northeast. To approach this end, he sought to sustain an independent foreign policy in order to discourage the North Vietnamese from exploiting their long established links with the Pathet Lao.[9] Initial success in negotiations with Pathet Lao representatives in August 1956 was followed by visits to Hanoi and Peking. These visits were symbolic rather than substantive and, although they took place in a cordial atmosphere, they did not result in formal diplomatic recognition. Souvanna Phouma conceded no more than that his country had no need of the protection of SEATO, and insisted that it should continue to accept American aid, provided from 1955. This position was no different in principle from that of Cambodia which appeared to be tolerated by China and the United States. However, while the international orientation of Laos under Souvanna Phouma produced a warm response from the Communist powers, Thailand and the United States were much less sympathetic and interpreted what was no more than a marginal shift in foreign policy as an indication of a major increase in Communist influence.[10]

Negotiations in detail with the Pathet Lao proceeded laboriously from August 1956 until November 1957, by which time the National Assembly approved agreements to establish a Government of National Union (to incorporate a Pathet Lao component), to reunify the country and to observe a foreign policy of neutrality. With apparent agreement on an internal balance, there followed a polarization of internal political forces which looked outside the country for support — speedily forthcoming in the case of the West. This process of polarization was stimulated by the outcome of supplementary elections held in May 1958, in which the Neo Lao Hak Xat (Lao Patriotic Front) — the political arm of the Pathet Lao and its allies — made a strong showing, in part because of economic disparities induced by the American aid programme. One consequence of left-wing electoral success was the emergence of a new political organization based on the army and the bureaucracy which described itself as the Committee for the Defence of National Interests (CDNI). It has been explained that: 'It was the first organization in Laos that could sensibly be called "right-wing" and its formation marked the polarization of political forces in cold war terms. It could be said that both the United States and the Communists now had front organizations in Laos'.[11]

The emergence of the CDNI, with substantial American support, served to reverse the trends initiated by Souvanna Phouma, who was forced from office. In August 1958 a new government was formed, led by Phoui Sananikone, which included four members of the CDNI but excluded any representation from the Lao Patriotic Front. This internal political transformation was reflected immediately in foreign policy. Lip service only was paid to non-alignment. The practical orientation of the new government was towards the United States and also Thailand, whose military leadership had close associations with the CDNI.

The internal rupture meant the end of any prospect, however tenuous, of political coexistence within Laos. It marked also a turning point in the reinvolvement of Laos in the wider conflict in Indochina. Politics had come to an end and the Pathet Lao were faced with the alternative of armed struggle to stake a claim to participate in the overall political direction of the country. In this objective, they found ready support from their North Vietnamese mentors who regarded Laos with proprietary regard and also as a point of entry to South Vietnam. International tension rose in late July 1959 when the Laotian government alleged that there had been an invasion by North Vietnam in Sam Neua Province and, in successive months called on the United Nations for assistance. In consequence, the United States stepped up its military assistance. Internally, the influence of the army increased and in April 1960 the CDNI consolidated its political position through electoral manipulation. The external alignment of Laos was reaffirmed, despite formal adherence to a policy of neutrality, which in turn drew a hostile response in Hanoi and Peking.

A dramatic attempt to revive a more substantive non-alignment, but one which produced further political and physical fragmentation, occurred in August 1960 when a young paratroop officer, Captain Kong Lé, mounted a coup in Vientiane.[12] Kong Lé's aims were simply expressed. He sought a return to a genuine neutrality and the end of internecine conflict and corrupt administration. Souvanna Phouma was called back to head a government and he sought, at the outset, to restore the internal political balance through negotiations with the Pathet Lao and to ensure in consequence the recognized neutral status of Laos. But these efforts were to no avail as right and left-wing forces, encouraged by their external backers, assumed irreconciliable positions.

The Thais gave strong support to the CDNI luminary and Defence Minister Phoumi Nosovan (a relative of Thai Premier, Sarit) who ensconced his forces in the south of the country (assisted by American logistical facilities and military supplies) and then launched a successful assault on Vientiane during December 1960. The outcome of this internal confrontation was total confusion in the foreign relations of Laos. In September Souvanna Phouma's government had established diplomatic relations with Moscow and subsequently secured material assistance, including petroleum, from the Soviet Union which offset the effects of a Thai economic blockade. Shortly before the fall of Vientiane, Souvanna Phouma had gone into exile in Cambodia, though retaining still the recognition of Moscow. The Western Powers and Thailand, however, transferred their recognition to the new government in Vientiane led by Prince Boun Oum and Phoumi Nosovan. Kong Lé's neutral force retired to occupy the north-central Plain of Jars, to be stiffened by Pathet Lao units and North Vietnamese advisers and reinforced with arms and ammunition despatched by Soviet airlift. The governments of North Vietnam and China also recognized Souvanna Phouma, but lent support to the internal cause of the Pathet Lao.

In such circumstances of political and physical fragmentation, which resembled the closing stages of the First Indochina War, foreign relations as conventionally understood ceased to have meaning. Laos contained three politico-military groupings, each with its own sphere of territorial control and each abetted by external sponsors concerned to promote the internal and the international legitimacy of its respective client. Foreign policy *per se* had limited reference to a situation where the state of Laos existed only in terms of international legal fiction. At this point a diplomatic initiative from the Soviet Union received United States support because of the danger of an escalation in the internal conflict. In consequence, a fourteen power international conference on Laos was convened in May 1961 following a cease-fire agreement. The external sponsors of the competing Laotians were obliged to wait until June 1962, however, for a preliminary agreement between the three internal faction leaders, Souvanna Phouma, Souphanouvong, and Phoumi Nosovan (hastened by the defeat of the latter's forces at Nam Tha in May) before the conference could procede to an accord on a tripartite political coalition and international neutraliz-ation. Such was the formal international position of Laos on 23 July 1962 when the conference in Geneva concluded its deliberations.

## The Foreign Policies of the Aligned States

### THE PHILIPPINES
The Korean War led to a radical reappraisal of American security policy in Asia and, in consequence, the Philippines obtained a defence commitment for which the abortive Pacific Pact, proposed in 1949, would have been a feeble substitute. Adherence to the Defence Treaty of August 1951 reaffirmed the international orient-ation of the Philippines. Although free of any immediate challenge to external security, the anti-Communist and Catholic-induced political attitudes of the Filipino élite was such that any serious alternative in foreign policy was not contemplated. The United States was perceived as the natural guardian of the Philippine State and presidential candidates sought endorsement and funds from that source. There is no doubt that the American Embassy encouraged this attitude and is known to have played an active part in sponsor-ing the successful candidature of Ramon Magsaysay in November 1953. Although Magsaysay cannot be described as a servile client of the United States where the domestic interests of his country were concerned, his presidency was characterized by a foreign policy tied to close association with Washington.[13] For example, the Philippines was an automatic, if subordinate candidate for membership in the American-inspired Southeast Asia Treaty Organization established in Manila in September 1954.

During the middle 1950s the relationship with the United States was not free from strain in its bilateral aspect, but any differences which occurred did not affect the international position of the Philippines. On key foreign policy issues, the Philippines followed the lead of Washington. Although fairly wide-ranging diplomatic ties were established in Asia (e.g. with India, Indonesia, and Cambodia), its primary Asian links were with Taiwan, South Vietnam, and

Thailand. Any hopes held of acting as 'a bridge of understanding' between Asia and the West on the basis of situation, history, and culture were misfounded and unrealized. The Filipinos enjoyed little prestige and were perceived in terms of the unfortunate label of President Taft, 'little brown brothers', denied a true Asian identity because of the paternalistic association with the United States. At Bandung, where the Philippine delegation was charged by the United States to be an anti-Communist spokesman, an attempt was made to demonstrate the rectitude of the Philippine's international outlook, an exercise which found greater favour with Chou En-lai than with Jawaharlal Nehru.[14]

The all-embracing relationship with the United States did not meet with unqualified approval within the Philippines. Among Filipino politicians, Senator Claro Recto in particular gave expression to resentment of a suffocating association which, it was alleged, denied the Philippines a rightful opportunity of realizing an Asian identity. Recto was in advance of his time in many of the views which he advocated, but he did strike a genuine chord. However, for those responsible for the foreign policy of the Philippines, any repudiation of the critical link with the United States was out of the question. This was especially the viewpoint of Magsaysay. Nonetheless, he was not unwilling to seek a revision of the terms of that link to Philippine advantage. During his presidency, cut short by his untimely death in 1957, trade relations, jurisdiction over military base areas, and the nature of the American defence commitment were discussed and questioned. Underlying much of the questioning was a sense of neglect on the part of the United States, exemplified in the level of economic and military assistance received in comparison with that dispensed to other countries and also in a resentment that past promises over war damages and payments to ex-servicemen had been only partially honoured. In the process of negotiations, some concessions were made by the United States. For example, in June 1954 a joint United States-Philippines Defence Council was created to meet criticisms of the institutional form of the Defence Treaty of 1951, while in December that year, the Laurel-Langley Trade Agreement assisted economic prospects, acknowledged sovereign control of the peso and modified the symbolic irritant of the parity rights issue.

Such bilateral modification of relationship had no significant impact on the place of the Philippines in the Asian world. It was only with the presidency of Carlos Garcia from 1957 to 1961 that initiatives were taken outside the special association with the United States to promote an independent role in Asia. This materialized in July 1961 with the establishment of the Association of Southeast

Asia (ASA) in co-operation with Malaya and Thailand. This body represented a modest undertaking and achievement. It was cast solely in economic and cultural terms, but had no adherents other than a fellow member of SEATO and a newly independent state in defence association with Britain. If the Philippines had sought an opening to Asia, the outcome was an association with like-minded Western-oriented states with closely identified views on Communism and the way to seek security from its challenge. Although at the beginning of the 1960s, the Philippines was tentatively feeling its way to a more independent international position, it was unwilling to repudiate the cornerstone of its foreign policy — its close alignment with the United States.

THAILAND

Thailand had been the first country in Asia to contribute troops to the United Nations command in Korea. This initiative marked the end of any prior equivocation over alignment, while a sense of vulnerability arising from Thailand's geopolitical situation in mainland Southeast Asia was moderated by tangible American appreciation of the Thai military involvement. At this stage, the association between Thailand and the United States did not find expression in a formal defence pact, although this was the goal of the government in Bangkok which consistently sought more assured access to countervailing power against a Communist threat.

The political orientation of the government in Bangkok manifested itself in an obsessive concern with this threat, although, in effect, the major challenges to political order during the 1950s arose from factional rivalry within the country's armed forces. Concern with Communist threats appeared to be better founded during the closing stages of the First Indochina War. During 1953 the Viet-Minh penetrated into Laos and also Cambodia and repeated the intervention in the following year. Also, the Chinese government announced the establishment of a T'ai Autonomous People's government in Yunnan Province, which received the vocal endorsement of the deposed and exiled Premier Pridi Phanomyong who appeared in Peking in July 1954. The course of the war in Indochina revived fears of traditional conflict with the Vietnamese over boundaries of influence along the Mekong Valley. The Chinese initiative was equally alarming. It suggested a subversive challenge to the integrity of the Thai state.

After the Indochina settlement at Geneva, there was no question of Thailand toying with a neutralist policy. It had not been represented at the meeting of the Colombo Powers in 1954 but, instead, had brought the Viet-Minh intervention into Laos to the attention of the United Nations Security Council. By this stage, the Thai government was most anxious to secure from its allies the military guarantee that had not been forthcoming during the Korean War. Accordingly, Thailand was enthusiastic about membership of SEATO, which meant a formal military alliance with the United States, even though the global strategy of that country did not then permit the stationing of ground forces on the mainland of Asia. Such an alliance brought considerable material benefits, especially to the military establishment which dominated the government of Thailand.

Thailand had entered into formal alliance with an extra-regional power as a member of an organization designed as an instrument for the containment of China. By such commitment, Thailand disassociated itself from those newly independent Asian states which rejected alignment as an approach to security. However, Thailand did send a delegation to Indonesia in April 1955 for the Asian-African Conference. Its Foreign Minister, Prince Wan, met the Chinese Prime Minister, Chou En-lai, and received his assurances of peaceful intent, together with explanations of Pridi's presence in Peking and the purpose of the T'ai minorities government in Yunnan. Prince Wan was invited to Peking for discussions on the citizenship and status of overseas Chinese in Thailand who had been subject to increasing restrictions by the government in Bangkok. The Thai Foreign Minister was content to receive assurances from Chou En-lai, and neither responded to the invitation to visit Peking nor indicated any change in his country's international position.

The spirit of Bandung reflected a general easing of international tensions, which found significant expression in the great power talks at Geneva in July 1955. In August 1955 informal discussions took place also in Geneva between representatives of the United States and the Chinese People's Republic. This event had repercussions within Thailand, where it was construed as an erosion of the alliance upon which national security was based. The immediate dilemma for Thailand was how to reinsure against American equivocation from a position of potential vulnerability and to take the edge off Chinese hostility. In the absence of any dramatic reappraisal of American policy, the Thai reaction was to sustain the alliance association but also to soften its unofficial face to China. For example, trade restrictions were eased and unofficial visits by Thais to China were not obstructed where it suited governmental purpose.

In the mid-1950s, the public atmosphere of Thai politics was transformed as Marshal Phibun sought to import Western styles in order to seek a popular mandate in open elections. Such democratic excesses (by Thai standards) came to a sudden and dramatic halt during 1957 in the aftermath of a general election which, in effect, rejected Phibun's leadership. In September the army, led by its commander, Sarit Thannarat, intervened and re-established an even more authoritarian political order. He subsequently reaffirmed Thailand's commitment to SEATO and the aligned nature of its foreign policy. This stand coincided with a hardening of Chinese international attitudes in the crisis over the offshore islands in the Taiwan Straits. Other factors of significance affecting Sarit's position were the agreement to permit Pathet Lao participation in government in Laos, the subsequent success of its political arm in supplementary elections, and also the Cambodian diplomatic recognition of Peking in July 1958. Events in Laos in particular were to become of increasing importance in the foreign relations of Thailand in the next decade.

During the 1950s Thai foreign policy was geared to the association with the United States. Within the framework of that association, there took place a measure of response and adaptation to the changing international position of China and to the prospect of any policy reappraisal by the United States. However, by the end of the decade a policy of alignment was reasserted without equivocation.[15]

THE REPUBLIC OF (SOUTH) VIETNAM

In the immediate aftermath of the Geneva settlement of July 1954 the truncated state of Vietnam south of the seventeenth parallel did not appear to have a future as a separate entity. Its Prime Minister, Ngo Dinh Diem, had returned from an expatriate existence to form a cabinet in June, much too late to have any impact on the proceedings in Geneva, although he refused to be bound by the accords reached there.

Foreign policy for the Diem government was geared essentially to the problems and needs of internal political consolidation. Its principal preoccupations were the preservation of the lower half of Vietnam as a separate political entity and the attainment of international status through the recognition of other states. In these two aims, Diem initially achieved more than just a measure of success. Internal political consolidation was attained within a very short period of time and as a consequence confidence was added to determination to deny the requests of the North Vietnamese government for discussions on holding country-wide elections by July 1956, as provided in the Geneva settlement. Diplomatic recognition was obtained in time from approximately sixty states, a product of the special association with the United States.

Before Diem assumed power he had been impressed by the philosophy of non-alignment but, faced with the vulnerable condition of South Vietnam, he felt obliged to secure effective countervailing power against the North.[16] He was confirmed in this by his long standing anti-Communism. With the abdication of the French, and what he regarded also and always as their treachery, he turned to the United States, whose government committed itself to him unequivocally by May 1955. Consequently, the United States became the political patron of South Vietnam and provided substantial quantities of economic aid and military assistance. The relationship between the representatives of the United States and Diem was often difficult and strained, as his style of government was often repugnant to his patrons. But they were prepared to tolerate and sustain his regime as long as he was successful.

In the middle 1950s it was common to read and hear South Vietnam described as a political miracle, particularly after the outbreak of peasant revolt in the North. But by the end of the decade, because of the insurgency feeding off economic grievance and repressive internal policies, disillusion began to set in and the relationship with Washington became subject to increasing strain. The United States did not relent in its commitment to the political integrity and separate viability of the Republic of Vietnam, but it held undoubted reservations about the efficacy of the Diem government in view of its evident political failings. Indeed, it is claimed that in November 1960 the American Embassy in Saigon did not trouble to warn Diem of an abortive coup of which it had advance knowledge.[17] Under President Kennedy, the United States stepped up its military efforts to uphold the separate existence of the South, but its commitment to Diem diminished during the Buddhist agitation of 1963. The episode led to the withdrawal of American support and the direct involvement of the Kennedy Administration in the coup of November 1963 which resulted in Diem's assassination and the assumption of power by the military.[18]

THE DEMOCRATIC REPUBLIC OF (NORTH) VIETNAM

At Geneva, the representatives of the Viet-Minh had to be satisfied with only partial success. They assumed the government of Vietnam north of the seventeenth parallel and appeared content to accept the provision for country-wide elections to be held within two years. Their forces were withdrawn from Cambodia; in Laos their affiliate, the Pathet Lao, continued to exercise territorial control in the northeast.

The Democratic Republic of Vietnam (DRV) had received international recognition from other Communist states early in 1950. In 1954 the principal priorities of those who assumed power in Hanoi were to consolidate their internal position along conventional

Communist lines and to negotiate the reunification of the country with a government in the south which was not expected to endure.

The diplomacy of reunification was to be a total failure because of the unexpected success of the Diem government and also because the Geneva settlement had not provided international machinery for enforcement of its provisions. In July 1955 Hanoi announced its readiness to hold a consultative conference with the authorities in the south to prepare for general elections to realize the unity of Vietnam. Subsequent initiatives, which were continued through to the early months of 1956, were all to no avail, as Diem refused to negotiate. Messages to the co-chairmen of the Geneva Conference and vocal support from the Chinese People's Republic and the Soviet Union for a new conference to guarantee the implementation of the Geneva settlement of 1954 made no impact. After July 1956 the DRV government gave less public attention to reunification and more consideration to internal consolidation, especially the question of land reform which was to cause considerable peasant dissension.

In April 1955 Prime Minister Pham Van Dong, had participated in the new Communist diplomacy at Bandung. Assurances of peaceful intent were given to neighbouring states and respect was declared for their political integrity. In foreign relations, principal ties were with the Chinese People's Republic and the Soviet Union. Prior to Geneva, the Vietnamese Communists had received most consistent support from their Chinese comrades, while the Soviet Union had been equivocal. Nonetheless, in the light of historical experience and its geopolitical position, the DRV government sought to avoid placing itself in a position of undue dependence on its northern neighbour. Economic assistance was received from both the Soviet Union and China, although initially in greater amount from the latter. During the late 1950s, as the Sino-Soviet dispute developed, the question of avoiding undue and irreversible commitment became a major consideration in the foreign policy of North Vietnam.[19]

Although the priority of reunification appeared to have been reduced in 1956 it was revived with vigour by the ruling Lao Dong Party during 1959. At its Third Congress in September 1960 the strategic tasks of the Vietnamese revolution were announced as: 'Firstly, to carry out the socialist revolution in the North. Secondly, to liberate the South from the rule of the American imperialists and their henchmen, achieve national reunification, and complete independence and freedom throughout the country'. The following December brought the formation of the South Vietnam National Liberation Front which, although based on the participation of southern cadres, became the instrument of the northern government to secure its territorial aims.

MALAYA

By the middle of the 1950s most of the colonies in Southeast Asia had experienced a transfer of power and the successor states had begun on independent practice of foreign policy. A notable exception was Malaya where the Japanese surrender, although marked by inter-communal violence, was followed by an easy restoration of British control. Although some among the Malay community were influenced politically by Indonesian resistance to the Dutch, substantive nationalist organization did not emerge or take on challenging form until 1946 when the British sought to implement a plan for political unification which would have denied the formal sovereign position of the Malay sultans and provided easy access to equal citizenship for all domiciled in the projected Malayan Union, irrespective of racial identity.[20]

Vigorous Malay opposition to what was construed as a denial of an assumed birthright shook the initial complacency of the British colonial administration and led to a revision of proposals for constitutional change to accord more closely with Malay wishes. This done, there was an expectation of a measured progress towards self-government within the Malay peninsula, separated politically from the island of Singapore which still served as a British military base. Movement towards self-rule was interrupted in the peninsula, however, by the declaration of a state of emergency in June 1948 in the face of an insurrection launched by the Malayan Communist party. Full independence had to await the virtual quelling of this insurrection as well as the emergence of an inter-communal political coalition between Malays, Chinese, and Indians. In Singapore, a progressive extension of the franchise took place until in June 1959 internal self-government was attained.

Independence in Malaya was achieved in August 1957 with a minimum of friction between the nationalist leaders and the vacating colonial power. With independence, an agreement was concluded with Britain which covered external defence and also internal security against the Communist insurgents, who had retreated by this stage to the border with Thailand. The sense of security provided through the Anglo-Malayan Defence Agreement — with which Australia and New Zealand became associated — made it possible for independent Malaya to repudiate the idea of membership in SEATO, which might well have alienated a number of states in Asia with whom Malaya sought friendly relations, as well as suggesting to its sizeable Chinese community that the country was to become involved in an anti-Chinese combination.

The initial international outlook of the Malayan government was to play down the role of foreign policy. Tunku Abdul Rahman (who

assumed the office of Foreign Minister as well as Prime Minister)
refrained from startling initiatives and flamboyant rhetoric. Membership in the Commonwealth was never questioned; nor was the strong
residual link with Britain. And the personal associations of the Prime
Minister counted for much in this respect. Malaya was undoubtedly
anti-Communist, but not in any evangelical sense. However, a lack
of experience in foreign relations led to occasional actions which
produced irritation if not resentment on the part of some Asian
states.[21]

The independence of Malaya did not produce any radical dis-
continuities in foreign policy or any desire for great power entanglement beyond the association with Britain. From 1959 a mild
propensity to regional co-operation was manifested and achieved
limited fulfilment in 1961 in Malaya's membership of ASA in
company with Thailand and the Philippines. While not necessarily
perceived in the same client role as the Philippines, Malaya appeared
to be a Western-oriented state, without the conspicuous disadvantage of open alliance with the United States. Foreign relations were
portrayed by the Tunku as a pastime for gentlemen which should
not bear heavily on the priorities and resources of government. It
was only with the compelling desire to encapsulate, within a wider
federation, all of the former and existing British territories in
maritime Southeast Asia that the more abrasive realities of international life made themselves felt in Kuala Lumpur.[22]

Up to this point, we have considered the various transfers of power
in Southeast Asia together with the first faltering steps in the
independent practice of foreign policy by the new states. Most of
these fitted easily enough into the general analytical categories of
alignment and non-alignment. Such categories have a reference
point external to Southeast Asia. Consequently limited attention
has been given, so far, to the interaction of the new states with one
other in a regional context. It is this deficiency which the following
chapter will seek to repair.

References

1  For a comprehensive assessment of neutralism see Peter Lyon, *Neutralism*,
   Leicester, 1963.
2  William C. Johnstone, *Burma's Foreign Policy*, Cambridge, Mass., 1963,
   p. 66.
3  Quoted in Johnstone, *op. cit.*, p. 171.

4 See Daphne Whittam, 'The Sino-Burmese Boundary Treaty', *Pacific Affairs*, September 1961. For a more general account of Sino-Burmese relations see John H. Badgley, 'Burma and China: Policy of a Small Neighbour', in A. M. Halpern (ed.), *Policies Towards China: Views From Six Continents*, New York, 1965.

5 I have relied much in the following section on the writings of Herbert Feith to whom I, like so many, am greatly indebted, especially *The Decline of Constitutional Democracy in Indonesia*, Ithaca, 1962 and 'Dynamics of Guided Democracy' in Ruth T. McVey (ed.), *Indonesia*, New Haven, 1963.

6 For a vivid and agnostic account see G. H. Jansen, *Afro-Asia and Non-Alignment*, London, 1966. The optimism of the time is reflected by George McT. Kahin, *The Asian-African Conference*, Ithaca, 1956.

7 For an intellectual history and evaluation of such doctrine see George Modelski (ed.), *The New Emerging Forces, Documents on the Ideology of Indonesian Foreign Policy*, Canberra, 1963.

8 This section closely follows Michael Leifer, *Cambodia: The Search for Security*, New York, 1967.

9 See Paul F. Langer and Joseph J. Zasloff, *North Vietnam and the Pathet Lao*, Cambridge, Mass., 1970.

10 See E. H. S. Simmonds, 'The Evolution of Foreign Policy in Laos since Independence', *Modern Asian Studies*, April 1968, pp. 12–13.

11 *Ibid.*, p. 14.

12 For accounts of the circumstances of the coup and more general discussion of the domestic and international politics of Laos, see Hugh Toye, *Laos, Buffer State or Battleground*, London, 1968 and Arthur J. Dommen *Conflict in Laos*, New York (revised edition), 1971.

13 One authority writing of Magsaysay has commented: 'To them (the Americans), he was the vindication of the American ideological experiment in the Philippines'. M. W. Meyer, *A Diplomatic History of the Philippine Republic*, Hawaii, 1965, p. 165.

14 For an account of the Philippines at Bandung, see J. L. Vellut, *The Asian Policy of the Philippines 1954–61*, Canberra, 1965, pp. 22–6.

15 Useful accounts of this period in Thai foreign policy may be found in Frank C. Darling, *Thailand and the United States*, Washington, 1965; and Donald E. Nuechterlein, *Thailand and the Struggle for Southeast Asia*, Ithaca, 1965.

16 William Henderson and Wesley R. Fishel, 'The Foreign Policy of Ngo Dinh Diem', reprinted in Wesley R. Fishel (ed.), *Vietnam: Anatomy of a Conflict*, Illinois, 1968, p. 194.

17 *Ibid.*, p. 218.

18 See *The Pentagon Papers*, pp. 158–232.

19 See P. J. Honey, *Communism in North Vietnam*, Boston, 1963.

20 James De V. Allen, *The Malayan Union*, New Haven, 1967.

21 See T. H. Silcock, 'The Evolution of Malayan Foreign Policy', *Australian Outlook*, April 1963, p. 47.

22 A good account of the practice of foreign policy in Malaya is to be found in Robert O. Tilman, 'Malaysian Foreign Policy: The Dilemmas of a Committed Neutral', *Public Policy*, Cambridge, Mass., 1967.

*Chapter Three*

# THE TEMPER OF INTRA-REGIONAL CONFLICT

By August 1957, with the independence of Malaya, the process of decolonization in Southeast Asia was virtually complete. With the exception of divided Vietnam, all of the independent states had acquired membership in the United Nations and, although they faced problems of internal political order, the prospect of colonial restoration was far removed. With the end of conventional colonial domination the new states had been obliged to adjust to new responsibilities and to make their own independent assessments of security needs. The Bandung Conference of April 1955 served to point up the change in political character of Southeast Asia and also to publicize the idea of a spirit of Asian brotherhood. For a limited period a hope prevailed that independence and an awareness of kindred feeling among ex-colonial states would promote a sense of wider community. Such a sentiment, however, did not prevent the emergence of different and conflicting orientations to foreign policy which divided the newly emancipated countries. For independence involved a degree of direct contact which did not always reproduce the spirit associated with the Bandung meeting.

Intra-regional discord in Southeast Asia has drawn strength from a variety of sources, including historical antagonisms which revived after the removal of colonialism. In addition, differences of personality and ideology as well as disputes over territory have disturbed international relations within the region, virtually from the outset of independence. This chapter will look at examples of the experience of such conflict.

*Cambodia and its Neighbours*
Prior to the establishment of a protectorate by France in 1863 Cambodia was in danger of total subordination by T'ai and Vietnamese. French colonial rule served as a cocoon within which Khmer

50

identity was preserved and enriched. But the withdrawal of the French after the Geneva settlement exposed Cambodia to direct contact with its traditional antagonists. The acquisition of Cambodian provinces by Thailand in 1941 with the support of Japan had served to revive such fears even before independence, while the French colonial policy of encouraging the migration and settlement of Vietnamese indicated the further prospect of a large-scale westward movement.

These historical experiences and the reality of its geographic situation were among the factors which encouraged the adoption of a foreign policy of non-alignment by Cambodia, particularly as its neighbours and traditional antagonists were aligned closely with the United States. Cambodia's practice of non-alignment served in turn to revive acrimonious relationships, albeit in modern form, as Thailand and South Vietnam came to view their common neighbour as some sort of Trojan horse within which Communist subversion could be nurtured to their disadvantage. In consequence, both countries were uninhibited in supporting illegal and exiled opposition groupings. Within Cambodia, the revival of old antagonisms was exploited and even encouraged in order to assist the domestic political purposes of a personal leadership. Concurrently, a strong sense of vulnerability on the part of Cambodia and a deep resentment of the patronizing attitude of its more powerful and aligned neighbours produced a hypersensitive attitude to national security.

Cambodian-Thai antagonisms during the period of Prince Sihanouk's dominance reflected the differing perceptions with which the leaders of the two states looked at one another. This was demonstrated strikingly during the dispute over physical possession of a ruined Khmer temple situated on a contested border in the Dangrek mountains. Thai frontier guards had occupied the temple site just prior to Cambodian independence and, for Prince Sihanouk, Thai possession was a symbolic reminder of traditional subordination which he resented deeply. After fruitless requests for the restoration of the temple, the Cambodian government brought the matter before the International Court of Justice, an initiative which contributed to a breach in diplomatic relations in October 1961 that lasted until the fall of Prince Sihanouk in 1970. In June 1962 the World Court found in favour of Cambodia and the Thais gave up their tenure with reluctance and bitterness under pressure from the United States.

The dispute over the temple of Preah Vihear aggravated bad feeling between the two countries at the personal level which was reflected in name-calling and mutual irreverence. One demonstration of such pettiness occurred in December 1963 following the death of Thailand's Prime Minister, Marshal Sarit, when Prince Sihanouk declared a public holiday to celebrate the occasion. Thai leaders, especially former foreign minister, Thanat Khoman, viewed the Cambodia of Prince Sihanouk with a mixture of pained irritation and genuine alarm, especially when his policy of non-alignment gave way to one of accommodation to the Chinese and Vietnamese Communists. For Prince Sihanouk, the recurrent and sometimes contrived antagonism with Thailand served as a touchstone for his policy of neutrality and as a signal to the Communist powers in Asia of his good intentions. His political disposition reflected also a concern that Thailand might itself seek an accommodation with the Communist powers, in which circumstances Sihanouk envisaged that Cambodia would be at a serious political disadvantage.

Following the deposition of Prince Sihanouk and Vietnamese Communist intervention in Cambodia, there ensued a rapid restoration of diplomatic ties between Bangkok and Phnom Penh. However, the experience of the new relationship has not been without its strains. Initial Thai enthusiasm for the provision of military assistance was not to be matched by performance, as the government in Bangkok expressed second thoughts on the subject for quite practical reasons of self-interest.

Foreign policy differences also marked the relationship between Cambodia and the southern portion of Vietnam. Conflicts arose from contrasting responses to the Cold War, while in addition historical and cultural legacies bedevilled the association. For the Cambodians, the perception of threat from the Vietnamese has been much more acute than that from the more culturally akin Thais. Experience of an inexorable movement of Vietnamese people in search of fertile rice lands at the expense of the old Khmer kingdom indicated a longstanding challenge to political existence and to cultural identity. Here too, personal factors entered into the relationship. Ngo Dinh Diem had an ill-concealed contempt for Sihanouk which was reciprocated in good measure.

Specific conflicts arose from Cambodian charges that the minority policies of the Saigon government were designed to eradicate the cultural identity of the substantial number of ethnic Khmers domiciled in South Vietnam. In addition matters of territorial possession, including the question of sovereignty over islands in the Gulf of Siam, aggravated an already embittered relationship. Indeed, at the outset of independence during the Geneva Conference on Indochina, the Cambodian representative reserved his government's position on a large tract of Cochinchina which was considered to be part of the Khmer heritage. The South Vietnamese for their part resented the equivocal course of Cambodian foreign policy. They were annoyed at Cambodia's willingness to provide political asylum to South Vietnamese dissidents and furious at the alleged use of Cambodian territory by Vietnamese Communist insurgents, a charge denied vehemently by Prince Sihanouk until 1968. In August 1963 diplomatic ties were broken on Cambodian initiative as a gesture of protest against the repression of Buddhist opposition by the Diem government. This breach was not repaired until after the overthrow of Prince Sihanouk in March 1970. An additional source of Cambodian rancour was the recurrent violation of Cambodian territory by South Vietnamese and American forces during the 1960s, often with tragic consequences for the civilian inhabitants. One such violation served in part to justify the Cambodian breach of diplomatic relations with the United States in May 1965.

Following the deposition of Prince Sihanouk, Cambodian-South Vietnamese relations were placed on a somewhat different footing. Factors of personality and ideology were set aside as South Vietnamese forces with American assistance intervened into Cambodia against their Communist counterparts. This alliance has been essentially a product of expediency and has been regarded in Cambodia as little more than an evil to be tolerated in order to repel a Communist invasion. The conduct of South Vietnamese troops inside Cambodia has been far from correct, for persons, property, and culture have been treated with less than respect and the post-Sihanouk relationship has been beset with considerable tension.

During the greater part of Prince Sihanouk's rule, Cambodian relations with Communist North Vietnam were characterized by strained amiability. With the withdrawal of the Viet-Minh after the Geneva Conference and the assurances provided by Pham Van Dong at Bandung, Prince Sihanouk concluded that there was little point in adopting policies which might antagonize the Vietnamese Communists, unless they gave cause for concern by their actions.

Initially, Cambodia did not enter into diplomatic ties with Hanoi but kept its distance. With the deterioration of relations with South Vietnam and the onset of insurgency there, commercial representatives were exchanged with North Vietnam. Fundamental to a progressive improvement in relations and an upgrading of representation was the growing conviction of Prince Sihanouk at the outset of the 1960s that South Vietnam was certain to succumb to the insurgency mounted by the National Liberation Front (NLF). In consequence, he moved to insure both with Peking and Hanoi out of an initial expectation that the Chinese government would be willing to interpose a protective presence to contain any Vietnamese Communist territorial ambitions in other parts of Indochina. In 1967, under the impact of an internal leftist insurgency in Cambodia,

Sihanouk felt obliged to come to terms directly with the Vietnamese Communists. In return for Cambodia's formal recognition of the National Liberation Front, described by Sihanouk as 'the sole authentic representative of the South Vietnamese people', he secured its public and written recognition of Cambodia's borders and a declaration of respect for the exisiting line of demarcation. The government in Hanoi followed suit. In June 1967 it was announced that a permanent diplomatic representation of the NLF would be set up in Phnom Penh and also that full diplomatic relations would be established with Hanoi. It was most probably following this package arrangement that a secret agreement was made whereby Cambodia provided port and transportation facilities for the entry of arms and supplies to the border region adjoining South Vietnam.

It is uncertain to what extent Prince Sihanouk was genuinely concerned about the growth of a Vietnamese Communist military establishment within Cambodia, but by early 1969 he had become increasingly vocal in his public criticism of that presence and by the middle of the year had re-established diplomatic relations with the United States. Although Cambodia accorded immediate recognition to the Provisional Revolutionary government of South Vietnam formed in June 1969, his public condemnation of the Vietnamese Communist presence was sustained and served ironically as the ostensible issue which precipitated his overthrow in March 1970. A preliminary to this episode was the inspired sacking of Vietnamese Communist diplomatic missions in Phnom Penh. Within two weeks the Vietnamese Communists withdrew all their diplomatic staff and an undeclared state of war came into existence. The fall of Sihanouk and the circumstances which surrounded that event was construed by the Vietnamese Communists as representing a radical transformation of the political orientation of Cambodia within Indochina and as a direct threat to their interests. They acted accordingly.[1]

Underlying the course of relations with North Vietnam has been the knowledge in Cambodia that the Viet-Minh had sought to sponsor an affiliated movement there during the First Indochina War. At the Geneva Conference, the initial position of Pham Van Dong had been to demand representation for a so-called Khmer Resistance government. This demand was withdrawn only after pressure from the Soviet and Chinese delegates. Although Viet-Minh forces withdrew from Cambodia after the Geneva settlement, an abiding suspicion remained that in time the Vietnamese Communists would seek to reconstitute Indochina under their dominion. Such a view may be unduly alarmist but it is plausible to assume that the Vietnamese Communists, who have never relented in their determination to unify the whole of Vietnam, would be concerned to ensure, at least, that any neighbouring regimes should not be ill-disposed in the event of attainment of that long denied goal.

Of all its neighbours, Laos has been of least direct concern for Cambodia. Laos has been important, however, as a test of American resolve and as an indicator for a reappraisal of its own foreign policy. It was during the period of the Geneva Conference on Laos, for which Prince Sihanouk had been a vigorous advocate, that Cambodian policy began to deviate from a strict non-alignment to a progressive accommodation to the Asian Communist powers.

Cambodia's relations with its neighbours exemplify interstate politics in Indochina. These have been the product of two dominant forces. First, traditional association and antagonism. In this case, ethnic identity and historical legacy have combined with geopolitical considerations to revive old enmities and conflicts within the peninsula. Secondly, modern ideology has interpenetrated traditional factors to aggravate longstanding antagonisms. The impact of ideology has reflected also the interests and involvements of extra-regional powers. While Cambodia maintained a substantive neutral position and Prince Sihanouk retained his position of political leadership, there existed a measure of symmetry between traditional antagonisms, rooted in ethnicity, and ideological conflict, linked to external alignment. Such was certainly the case with Cambodia's relations with its neighbours to west and east. After Prince Sihanouk's deposition, however, which provoked a polarization of political forces in Indochina, ethnic and traditional factors came to be less central to the conflict situation. Ranged against each other have been multi-ethnic forces divided by political ideas and modes of social organization. By this juncture, Cambodia's relations with her neighbours had become significantly transformed as a consequence of internal and external events.

*Indonesia Adopts 'Confrontation'*

Indonesia's recourse to confrontation marked a phrenetic phase in foreign policy which drew its character from the quality of domestic political life. After the breakdown of the parliamentary system and its replacement by Guided Democracy, foreign policy assumed an increasingly radical cast. The prime mover in foreign policy initiatives was President Sukarno who had changed the constitution in order to assume full power. He directed Indonesia away from the more conventional practice of non-alignment to join his country with what he described as the New Emerging Forces (Nefos). Such a grouping incorporated, according to him, the progressive elements of the world, including the Socialist/Communist countries and the ex-colonial states who were represented as ranged against the Old Established Forces of imperialism and colonialism.[2]

Confrontation involved a style of bellicosity which reflected the changing priorities of Indonesian foreign policy and the flavour of Guided Democracy. It was an attempt, in part, to promote the diplomatic isolation of an antagonist by attaching to it a label that other progressively minded states would regard as tainted. It was an attempt to intimidate to gain political ends by skirting the brink of hostilities in a context where enemy retaliation would only assist the cause of internal political solidarity. Confrontation as an expression and as a mode of activity had been successfully utilized to put increased pressure on the Netherlands to relinquish West Irian during 1960–62. In that episode threats, bluster, and limited military activity served to create an international climate which prompted the United States to intervene to effect a Dutch withdrawal in August 1962 lest the Communists, domestic and international, profit from the situation.[3] Its more striking manifestation took place in January 1963 when the Foreign Minister, Dr Subandrio, adopted it publicly as the policy of Indonesia towards the Federation of Malaya, then engaged in promoting the wider entity of Malaysia through the incorporation of Singapore and British North Borneo. This policy was not reversed officially until August 1966.

The idea of a Malaysia was of long standing but emerged as a practical proposition when it was endorsed in May 1961 by Tunku Abdul Rahman, the Prime Minister of Malaya. His prime purpose in adopting the idea was to bring about the political encapsulation of the self-governing and predominantly Chinese populated island of Singapore within a wider federal union on the understanding that the non-Chinese majority of the inhabitants of the British Borneo territories would more than compensate in racial terms, for the inclusion of Singapore. This initiative brought a positive response both from the British government and also from that of Singapore, which had campaigned publicly and privately for a union with Malaya.

The initial Indonesian reaction to the proposal to amalgamate Malaya, Singapore, and the British Borneo territories, while in no way sympathetic or encouraging, was muted rather than hostile. The relationship between Indonesia and Malaya had been uneasy for the few years of Malayan independence and it reflected in part the differing orientation and style of political leadership in the two countries. Nonetheless, in the months following the Tunku's initiative and before it was apparent that the scheme would be implemented, the Indonesian position was correct diplomatically.

One reason for this rectitude was that the political energies of the Republic were being channelled in confrontation against the Dutch, who refused to concede West Irian until August 1962. Through 1962 preparations for the establishment of Malaysia continued without major external obstacle, although in the middle of the year the Philippines laid a formal claim to the territory of North Borneo (Sabah).

Indonesia's attitude of unenthusiastic acceptance, more evident after the West Irian settlement, continued until December 1962 when a revolt occurred in the British protected state of Brunei which, at the time, was a candidate for membership within Malaysia. The uprising was represented by its leaders as a demonstration of opposition to the formation of Malaysia and they demanded, in its stead, a separate political union of all three territories of northern Borneo. The anti-colonial aspect of the revolt, which was not a complete surprise to the Indonesian government, dovetailed well with the prevailing temper of Indoresian politics and brought above the surface the reservations held in Jakarta about the Malaysia scheme. The immediate reaction of the Indonesian government was to express publicly its sympathy for the Brunei revolt which in turn provoked a retort from the Malayan government. A series of acrimonious exchanges led to a statement by Dr Subandrio on 20 January 1963 that 'in view of Malaya's unfriendly attitude, Indonesia could no longer maintain a passive attitude but must pursue with firmness a policy of confrontation'.

The Brunei revolt, which was crushed within days, served as the precipitating cause for Indonesia's vigorous opposition to the formation of Malaysia, but the sources of the ensuing conflict lay elsewhere.[4] To begin, there was the factor of mutual perception. The political experience and orientation of Indonesia was totally dissimilar to that of Malaya and in the context of Guided Democracy the differences in political style tended to be dramatically highlighted. The Sukarno regime was committed to the view that an authentic independence could only follow from a revolutionary struggle with a colonial power. Such a struggle had not been the experience of Malaya which had enjoyed a relatively benevolent tutelage at the hands of the British. According to the logic of Sukarno, Malayan independence was suspect.

Differences in political experience were matched by differences in political outlook and also in the form of the two regimes. Indonesia adhered in idea if not in practice to socialism, while Malaya was committed unashamedly to capitalist enterprise. Indonesia had expelled Dutch nationals and expropriated their assets in 1957 while British involvement in the Malayan economy was encouraged.

Opposition to Malaya and the projected Malaysia was justified, therefore, on the grounds that alien economic control meant that a disguised colonialism (neo-colonialism) was masquerading as an independent state in close proximity to Indonesia. In addition, the presence of foreign military bases within such a state was said to represent a threat to Indonesia's security.

Apart from differences of political experience, orientation and practice, there were other sources of discord. Indonesian memories of Dutch attempts to promote the play of centrifugal political forces during the revolutionary period had been revived during the regional uprisings of 1958 which centred on Sumatra and Sulawesi (Celebes). During this abortive episode, there was reason to believe that governments in Singapore and Malaya were sympathetic to the cause of the dissidents. Arms were provided through British controlled territories close to Indonesia, while the government of Malaya provided political asylum to some participants in the uprisings. Although a Treaty of Friendship between Indonesia and Malaya was signed in Kuala Lumpur in April 1959 the circumstances of the regional revolts continued to impair relationships. Resentment also existed over the economic dominance exercised by the port and commercial centre of Singapore, and especially over the role of capital controlled by the ubiquitous overseas Chinese community in Singapore and Indonesia. Singapore had long served as an entrepôt for Indonesian exports and also for raw materials smuggled out of the country. Its involvement in the latter activity had assisted the drain of foreign exchange from the exchequer of the government in Jakarta.

Indonesian attitudes to the overseas Chinese of Singapore and Malaya were complex. Resentment of their economic role was matched by an apprehension of their subversive potential at a time when a resurgent China was making an increasing impact in Asia. In spite of the radical orientation of the government of Sukarno in international relations, the Chinese People's Republic was viewed by Indonesia's military leaders with more than a measure of reserve. The prospect of Malaya (whose population was 37 per cent Chinese and whose economy was dominated by this community) forming a political junction with the predominantly Chinese island of Singapore and then extending this association to the very border of Indonesia in Kalimantan (Borneo) was contemplated with some alarm. It was argued that should Malaysia ever succumb to internal Chinese Communist takeover and become in consequence a client of the People's Republic, then Indonesia's security would be threatened directly. A related and more common feeling was a strong resentment that major territorial transfers in the close vicinity of a country of Indonesia's significance could be planned and executed without its approval.

Of all the factors which influenced the prosecution of confrontation, perhaps none had greater import than the character of Guided Democracy. Based on an associative and competitive triangular relationship between President Sukarno, the Indonesian Army, and the Indonesian Communist Party (PKI) the political system of Guided Democracy was characterized by its great stress on popular mobilization, exhortation, and nationalist heroics. Within this uneasy relationship which materialized in the late 1950s, Sukarno served as the fount of ideological wisdom and initiative and utilized the mass support proffered by the PKI to underpin his political position. At the same time demonstrable nationalist fervour and support for the doctrinal orthodoxies of Sukarno became an essential qualification for participants in the closed but competitive political process. Given the emerging ideological junction between Sukarno and the Communists, the army, which had experienced decreasing popular regard and a challenge to its *raison d'être* with the resolution of the West Irian conflict, had every reason to demonstrate its nationalist credentials. It was logical for its generals to support a venture like confrontation which would restore its prominence and also justify its large budget at a time of economic decline.

The PKI, long suspicious and apprehensive of the intentions of the army and dependent on the political patronage of Sukarno, experienced no conflict of interests in denouncing the Malaysia scheme when it was portrayed publicly in Malaya as a bulwark against Communism. There was the expectation, also, that confrontation might accelerate the drift of internal political events from which the PKI might well benefit. Sukarno, for his part, rejected and denounced Malaysia as a neo-colonial construct designed to bring about an imperialist encirclement of Indonesia. There is a school of thought which attributes Sukarno's attitude to Malaysia to a longstanding personal ambition to unify politically under Indonesian rule all the ethnic Malay peoples of Southeast Asia.[5] But irrespective of any territorial ambitions, which he never articulated after independence, Sukarno's opposition to Malaysia arose out of the structure of Indonesian political order. He owed his position within that order to a rejection of values associated with conventional political and economic practice. He sought to justify such a position by sustaining a political culture in which romanticism and agitational modes were stressed. After the settlement of the West Irian claim, Sukarno was faced with the prospect of returning Indonesia to a more quiescent internal existence, encouraged by the conditional promise of foreign aid from a Western consortium.

Such a reversion would have involved a threat to his political pre-eminence because the qualities and skills to be esteemed in such a context would be the opposite of those in which Sukarno excelled. Sober pragmatism was not his forte. It was alien to his temperament. His world was one filled with romantic symbols and mass exhortation. He thrived on a phrenetic political climate which he fostered assiduously with the backing of the PKI. The prospect of Malaysia and the revolt in Brunei provided an opportunity to sustain the values of Guided Democracy and his personal position. Confrontation enabled him to give continued emphasis to exhortation and to avoid the pressing problems of a deteriorating economy.

Confrontation assumed the form of a combined diplomatic and military campaign whose function was only in part to intimidate. A primary objective was to challenge the credentials of Malaysia as a state on the grounds that it represented a neo-colonialist conspiracy.

The military side of confrontation involved harrassment and the use of terror by guerrilla groups in North Borneo composed of Indonesian regular soldiers plus insurgents recruited in the main from the overseas Chinese community of Sarawak. Such tactics were intensified after the formal proclamation of Malaysia in September 1963 and the diplomatic breach between Jakarta and Kuala Lumpur. They were extended across the Straits of Malacca in August 1964 after the breakdown of talks in Tokyo aimed at securing a settlement. The military side of confrontation did not represent a major undertaking by Indonesia. Nonetheless, it required fifty thousand or more British and Commonwealth forces to contain it in such a way as to avoid the need for action against its source in Indonesia. When Indonesian aircraft dropped detachments of paratroops in peninsular Malaya, the response was not merely to bring the matter before the United Nations Security Council, but to threaten a naval-air strike in retaliation.

The process of limited insurgency was a sanction behind the diplomatic campaign against the new federation. This campaign was conducted concurrently with intermittent negotiations between the antagonists which took place in Manila, Bangkok, and Tokyo. Prior to the formation of Malaysia, Indonesia had sought to forestall its creation. After its establishment, Indonesia sought to coerce Malaysia to return to its interpretation of the spirit of an agreement reached between Sukarno and the Tunku in Manila in August 1963 on the determination of opinion in northern Borneo. Such a response would have confirmed that Indonesia had a legitimate right to be a principal party to territorial changes in its close vicinity. With the failure of this policy in Tokyo in June 1964,

Indonesia then sought to secure the excommunication of Malaysia from Third World congregations. In this endeavour, Indonesia was successful in denying Malaysia a place at the Second Conference of Non-Aligned Countries held in Cairo in October 1964. However, the public posture of Sukarno and his attempt to impose his concept of New Emerging Forces on the Conference succeeded only in alienating the leaders of the more conventional non-aligned states. Indonesia's abrupt withdrawal from the United Nations in January 1965 in protest at Malaysia's assumption of a one-year place on the Security Council worked also to impede the policy of isolating the new federation. Even the tenth anniversary celebrations of the historic Bandung Conference which were held in Jakarta in April 1965 did not produce the desired condemnation of Malaysia by the assembled delegates. The fiasco of the abortive Afro-Asian Conference, which was to have convened in Algiers in June 1965 and which Indonesia contemplated as a forum from which Malaysia could be excluded, dashed any hopes that might have been entertained about a formal denunciation of Malaysia as a pariah among the new states.

Through the year 1965 the process of confrontation lost momentum as contending political forces within Indonesia became increasingly absorbed in preparations for resolving the succession to Sukarno who was reported to be in ill-health. At the beginning of October an abortive coup was mounted which was attributed by the army to the PKI whose legal existence was brought to an end together with the life and liberty of many of its members by March 1966. The response of the army, led by Lieutenant-General, later President, Suharto resulted in a fundamental restructuring of the Indonesian political system to the great disadvantage of its other major elements. By the middle of 1966, with Sukarno removed from executive position, confrontation had become decreasingly relevant to internal political needs and could be abandoned without serious political disadvantage by the army.[6] At the same time, a recognition that the country could not continue to live off vacuous rhetoric encouraged the practice of a more modest and less abrasive foreign policy, one which would assure, in particular, access to foreign aid and investment.

Following negotiations in Bangkok and then in Jakarta, confrontation was brought to a formal close with an agreement in August 1966. The change of regime produced a radical change in international orientation. Relations with the Communist powers deteriorated, in particular those with the Chinese People's Republic, while co-operation was later undertaken with former antagonist Malaysia in joint military action against overseas Chinese insurgents along a common border in North Borneo. One year later, in August

1967, Indonesia and Malaysia co-operated in establishing the Association of Southeast Asian Nations (ASEAN) which reflected the transformation in international outlook in Jakarta.

### The Philippines and Sabah[7]

A third party to the somewhat abrasive diplomacy over the formation of Malaysia was the Philippines. This reputed client of the United States made a substantial, if temporary, impact within Southeast Asia as a consequence of its action to thwart the full establishment of the new federation.

The Philippines, under the Presidency of Diasdado Macapagal, had made formal objection in June 1962 to the proposed incorporation of the British colony of North Borneo within Malaysia. The territorial claim was based in part on the doubtful legality of the original British title to North Borneo which had been secured by private interests from the Sultanates of Brunei and Sulu in the late nineteenth century. Claims by Filipino heirs of the latter Sultanate to compound annual payments in return for the renunciation of proprietary rights lent colour and intrigue to the matter. For Macapagal the pursuit of the claim reflected personal ambition and a continuation of earlier efforts at securing *terra irredenta*. The initiative was also a means to give the Philippines a greater voice in regional affairs within Southeast Asia and to counter the widespread impression held of the Republic that it was merely a *de facto* dependency of the United States.

The promulgation of the claim during 1962 brought the Philippines initially into diplomatic conflict with Britain, then the sovereign power. Subsequently it involved the Philippines in an association with Indonesia to pressure the government of Malaya to reconsider the federal project.

The establishment of Malaysia on 16 September 1963 provoked a bitter and hostile response not only in Jakarta but also in Manila where the government refused to accord diplomatic recognition to the new federation. The immediate problem for the Philippines was that a transfer of power had taken place and that Malaysia had come into physical possession of Sabah. The Philippines did not enjoy any external source of support for its claim, except, perhaps, from Indonesia. And as Indonesia began to intensify the process of insurgency in the Borneo territories and then to launch sporadic incursions into the Malay peninsula during the latter part of 1964, Philippine political ardour for the association began to cool. Concurrently, domestic concern was expressed at the apparent leftwards drift of Indonesian politics and at the radical cast of its external associations, in particular the developing alignment with the Chinese People's

Republic, which crystallized in January 1965 with Indonesia's departure from the United Nations.

The claim to Sabah had been particularly associated with President Macapagal whose term of office expired in November 1965. By that time the internal political advantages of pursuing the claim were negligible and it did not bulk large in the presidential elections. Macapagal's victorious opponent, Ferdinand Marcos, had promised to restore full diplomatic relations with Malaysia if elected. This promise was fulfilled in June 1966 after some delays due to Indonesian pressure.

Diplomatic rapprochement improved the climate of relations between Manila and Kuala Lumpur, but did not produce a shift in the formal position of the Philippine government towards the claim. Although there was some indication of a desire to revive a working association that had been both cordial and fruitful in the recent past, evident reserve was demonstrated over any matter that seemed to question the validity of the claim. For example, in March 1967 the Philippine government was invited to send observers to witness the first direct elections to be held in Sabah, but refused to do so on the grounds that a despatch of observers might prejudice its position over the claim. Such indications of reserve did not, however, impede the participation of the Philippines with Malaysia in ASEAN in August 1967 and the following January, President Marcos and his wife made a state visit to Kuala Lumpur. Yet only two months after the state visit, the issue of the Sabah claim again erupted to sully relations between the two countries, for reasons connected with presidential politics and Muslim dissidence in the extreme south of the country.

During 1967 a number of Filipino Muslims had received training in insurgency techniques, allegedly for infiltration into Sabah, from a special military unit most probably authorized by the President himself. This enterprise became public knowledge in March 1968 following newspaper reports of a mutiny by some of the trainees at their camp on Corregidor Island. The Corregidor Affair, as it became known, was but one in a series of recurrent scandals that have enlivened the raucous political life of the Philippines. In Malaysia, the reports of the episode were received with great alarm. Demands for reassurance made to the Philippine government were met, however, with a public and official revival of the claim to Sabah and a presidential endorsement of a Congressional Act which redefined unilaterally the territorial extent of the Philippines to include Sabah. As a consequence, diplomatic relations were suspended, though without being broken formally. But following the unprecedented re-election of Marcos for a second term of office, their restoration was announced at the Third Ministerial Meeting of ASEAN held in Malaysia in December 1969.

The post-confrontation phase of the Philippine claim to Sabah, unfettered by association with Sukarno's Indonesia, pointed up a strain of compulsiveness in the Philippine conduct of foreign relations. The revelation of the Corregidor Affair and the associated revival of the claim to cover an evident embarrassment demonstrated an unusual order of priorities for a country that had appeared a natural ally of Malaysia in its approach to problems of regional security. President Marcos chose to make a policy decision which impaired the rapprochement with Malaysia and upset the progress of regional association to which all the members of ASEAN had paid public regard. The episode revealed a certain penchant for adventurism characteristic of the domestic style of Philippine politics before the introduction of martial law in September 1972. Such a penchant, which is, in part, a product of a sense of national deprivation arising out of the relationship with the United States, could well reassert itself in the future.

Since December 1969 the Philippine claim to Sabah has had occasional mention, but in muted tones. It has not been permitted to disturb a cautious relationship. Nonetheless, the legacy of the Corregidor Affair lingers still in the offices of the Malaysian Ministry of Foreign Affairs.

*Singapore and its Malay Neighbours*

Singapore became a fully independent state only in August 1965 when it separated involuntarily from Malaysia as a consequence of inter-communal tensions. This enforced secession took place a year before the formal end of confrontation between Indonesia and Malaysia, which was terminated to the sound of the proclamation of a common blood brotherhood between the two countries dominated politically by people of Malay stock. In consequence, Singapore experienced a strong sense of vulnerability, arising from its geopolitical position and racial composition, and in order to ensure permanence as an independent state took on politically many of the protective qualities of a hedgehog.

Numerous schemes had been advanced for the political unification of the Malay peninsula with Singapore, but none of these met with a positive response in Kuala Lumpur until 1961 when the prospect arose that the government of the island would fall into the hands of an extreme-leftist faction within the ruling People's Action Party (PAP). The process of negotiating the entry of Singapore into Malaysia was distinguished by hard bargaining and marred by ill-feeling. During the course of the negotiations, Lee Kuan Yew, the Prime Minister of what was still only a partially self-governing colony conducted himself as the head of government of a fully sovereign state: a pretension resented by the Malayan representatives. A clash of personalities was aggravated also by disagreement over the distribution of power within the projected federation. The Singapore Prime Minister was committed to the political union, but exploited the process of negotiations to represent himself as the stoic defender of the island's interests. Such a pose assisted the repair of his domestic political position weakened by dissidence and party defection, but sowed seeds for subsequent mistrust in Kuala Lumpur.

The government of Singapore, together with protagonists of the formation of Malaysia in North Borneo, was resentful at their exclusion from the tripartite negotiations in Manila in the middle of 1963. And when the Tunku agreed to postpone the inauguration of the new federation until after a determination of opinion by UN officials, the Singapore government protested vigorously. On 31 August 1963 — the day scheduled originally for the emergence of the new state — it was announced that Singapore would assume a *de facto* independence and that its Head of State would hold the defence and external affairs powers, until then exercized by the British, in trust for the central government of Malaysia pending the formation of the federation. This *coup de theatre*, which was related to the domestic politics of Singapore, as well as the unfinished bargaining over the island's terms of entry into Malaysia, caused great offence in Kuala Lumpur.

Such contention over the formation of Malaysia became overshadowed by the vigorous prosecution of confrontation by Indonesia and the rallying of all governments within Malaysia — federal and state — to the cause of national defence. Singapore experienced serious economic consequences from confrontation with the rupture of trade links by Indonesia, and was unable to compensate for this loss by securing the agreement of the federal government for a common market within Malaysia for manufactured products which it hoped to supply. At the root of an obviously uneasy relationship between Kuala Lumpur — the self-appointed Washington of Malaysia — and Singapore — depicted pointedly as the New York of the federation — was the barrier of communal differences between Malays and Chinese.

Emphasizing these differences were the stark contrasts of political style between government in Kuala Lumpur and Singapore, reflected in the performance of their leadership. An underlying suspicion was transformed into bitter conflict when Lee Kuan Yew entered his People's Action Party in the mainland Malayan elections of April 1964 in an unconcealed attempt to assume the non-Malay position held by the Malayan Chinese Association (MCA) in the intercommunal coalition federal government. This electoral intervention was a virtual failure, but its effect was to provoke Malay political feeling against the multi-racial advocacy of Lee, whose strident demand for 'a Malaysian Malaysia' was construed as an insidious plot to transform Chinese economic predominance in the country into political control. From this juncture relationships moved from bad to worse, with violence between Malays and Chinese occurring in Singapore in the autumn of 1964. A crisis point in both federal-state and intercommunal relations was reached with the decision by Lee in May 1965 to set up an opposition grouping, described as the Malaysian Solidarity Convention, which was committed to the attainment of a Malaysian Malaysia and which proclaimed collectively that it was not disposed to tolerate a situation where one race dominated the country.

The growing communal polarization finally led to the unilateral decision by the Malaysian Prime Minister in August 1965 that Singapore should separate from the federation to become an independent state. That such a separation could occur during the course of confrontation by Indonesia was an indication of the intensity of inter-communal feeling at the time.

An unhappy and stormy existence as a constituent part of Malaysia provided the background to Singapore's independent existence and conditioned the new state's approach to foreign relations. In the meantime, Indonesian confrontation continued to be directed at Singapore as well as at Malaysia. The small island state began its international existence as an encircled entity, distinguished from neighbouring antagonists by its ethnic identity and concerned lest any rapprochement between Indonesia and Malaysia take place at the expense of Singapore. Prime Minister Lee Kuan Yew articulated his fears shortly after separation, explaining: 'Our long term survival demands that there's no government in Malaysia that goes with Indonesia. Life would be very difficult if I found myself between Malaysia and Indonesia. Thus, I've no intention of making things difficult for the Tunku'.

In spite of such a self-denying ordinance, the subsequent relationship between Singapore and Malaysia was punctuated by acrimonious exchanges and episodes which indicate an underlying mistrust. In February 1966 a minor crisis arose when the Malaysian government sought to insist that one of its infantry battalions be retained on the island. At the time of separation, a principal fear of the Singapore government had been the recurrence of communal violence, especially in residential areas which had been the epicentre of such eruptions in 1964. It was to guard against such an eventuality that Malaysian troops remained in Singapore. The conflict, minor in itself, was resolved after much public argument. But the episode served to highlight the strongly-sensed vulnerability of Singapore. The correspondent of the London *Times* observed: 'Singapore's fear to put it bluntly was that the manoeuvre over these troops could have been the first step in a plot to overpower the independent island state'. Partially as a consequence of this episode it became impossible for the two governments to come to terms on defence arrangements as agreed in the separation document, despite public acknowledgement that the defence problems of the two states were indivisible.[8]

Tension between the two states revived during the latter part of 1966 after the end of Indonesian confrontation, which was negotiated without the participation of Singapore. Rapprochement between Indonesia and Malaysia was viewed with mixed feelings in the island state. And it was the prospect of an alignment to its disadvantage that prompted the government of Singapore to secure military advisers from Israel and to try to establish an independent defence capacity which would possess a potential for deterrence. This is not the place to discuss Commonwealth defence arrangements in Southeast Asia involving Singapore and Malaysia (see Chapter Five). It is important to stress, however, that irrespective of any subsequent willingness shown by Singapore to co-operate in such arrangements in association with Malaysia, an underlying concern with island defence against attack from its near neighbours has remained.

Singapore's relations with its other Malay neighbour have been characterized also by their abrasive quality. Diplomatic ties were established with Jakarta in August 1966 and vital trade links were re-established. The following year, Singapore joined with Indonesia and Malaysia — as well as Thailand and the Philippines — within ASEAN. Within this organization, the voice of Singapore has appeared to carry weight out of proportion to its intrinsic strength, and the quality of pragmatism which has distinguished the island state's practice of foreign policy has rubbed off on the functioning of the regional organization. However, an overriding aspect of Singapore's conduct of foreign relations has been a determined insistence that it should not be pressured by larger powers. This determination has been exemplified in relations with Indonesia. For example, at the end of October 1968, the Singapore government went ahead with the execution of two Indonesian marines who had been found guilty of sabotage and murder during the period of confrontation. This execution was a deliberate act of policy to demonstrate the determination of Singapore to defend its independence in every way. The immediate outcome of this action was an outbreak of violent demonstrations in Jakarta and elsewhere in Java against Singapore and local Chinese, while trade between the two countries was brought to a temporary halt. The episode could have seriously ruptured the recently repaired relationship but it was not permitted to do so by the Indonesian government which saw little profit in a renewal of past antagonisms. For its part, Indonesia has come to regard Singapore with pained irritation and has tried to overlook contrived diplomatic misdemeanours, such as the decision to send only a junior minister from Singapore to the conference on Cambodia which was held in Jakarta in May 1970. Indeed, Indonesia, which has no fear of tiny Singapore, has sought to present a benevolent face towards the island republic. One indication of a better level of understanding was the visit by Lee Kuan Yew to Indonesia in May 1973.

For Singapore, which stands in a different and asymmetrical relationship to Indonesia, there remains an underlying fear of what might ensue by way of adventurist policies should the present stable government in Jakarta be replaced by a more radically nationalist successor. In addition, it holds a collateral apprehension of dealing with a successful and strong Indonesia. It was in part for this reason that Singapore was pleased to be a member of ASEAN in the hope that this modest form of regional association might serve as a vehicle through which Indonesia could be accorded some form of primacy, as opposed to hegemony, with Southeast Asia.

## Two Potential Conflicts

Our discussion, so far, has centred on tangible and evident intraregional conflicts. Some of these appear to have been resolved, while others have only been set aside. However, we have not considered any dormant conflicts which, as yet, have not demonstrated much more than potential.

### THAILAND AND MALAYSIA

In the main, the post-independence relationship between Malaya/ Malaysia and Thailand has been cordial and co-operative. During his long tenure of office, much used to be made of the part-Thai parentage of Prime Minister Tunku Abdul Rahman, to exemplify the basis for good relations. There have been recurrent indications of co-operation between the governments in Bangkok and Kuala Lumpur in counter-insurgency operations along and across a common border. This common border which separates the two countries is not, however, of long standing. The four northern provinces of mainland Malaya, peopled in the main by Muslim Malays, were transferred from Thai to British jurisdiction as recently as 1909. During the rule of Phibun in the course of the Second World

War, his pan-Thai aspirations found expression in the enforced
reversion of these provinces to Thai administration in 1943, through
the good offices of the Japanese overlord. With the capitulation of
the Japanese, the four provinces were returned without delay to
British control. In practice, Thai administration had not had an
opportunity to make its presence felt. Nonetheless, the evidence of
expansionist intent has not been forgotten completely in Kuala
Lumpur, despite the current agreeable relationship.

If the experience of transfer of the four northern provinces of
mainland Malaya represents a source of unease in Kuala Lumpur,
then the character of the four southern provinces of Thailand
represents a source of apprehension in Bangkok. These provinces
were once part of the old Muslim state of Patani and were absorbed
within direct Thai administration at the turn of the twentieth
century. Their population of approximately three-quarters of a
million is predominantly Malay Muslim and in consequence a long-
standing concern has existed in Bangkok lest irredentist sentiment,
on either side of the common border with Malaysia, be exploited to
Thailand's territorial disadvantage. The basis for this concern is
not just the fact of ethnic affinity cutting across an international
border but the appearance in 1948 of a South Siam secession
movement.

Since 1948 the issue of Muslim separatism has remained dormant
but has revived in the 1970s. It has continued to trouble governments
in Bangkok who maintain a watchful eye on the activities of Malay
political organizations, especially in the Malaysian state of Kelantan.
The prospect of a renewal of irredentist activity has not been
allowed to disturb the inter-governmental relationship with Malaysia
which has continued to be cordial. And yet, despite such cordiality,
the Thais retain a near-surface sense of apprehension about its
potential and this apprehension is believed to be responsible, in part,
for problems of co-operation in counter-insurgency operations along
a common border against the military arm of the Malayan
Communist Party.

Although serious conflict over this issue is not anticipated, its
potential remains. For example, the matter bears on the internal
racial balance within Malaysia. The government of Malaysia is
Malay-dominated and communal violence in that country in May
1969 was linked directly to the question of whether such dominance
would continue to be exercized without challenge. For Malay
politicians concerned about the relationship between racial arithmetic
and political control, the natural northern boundary of Malaysia
would be along the line of ethnic settlement of the Muslim-Malays of
Thailand who would then be linked in political association with their

co-religionists to the south. Such an infusion of Malay numbers would make more certain a political predominance that was challenged in the elections of May 1969. The present government of Malaysia rules out such a solution to a domestic problem but the potential for conflict arising out of an international border cutting across ethnic patterns of settlement remains in the background of relations between two friendly neighbours.

THAILAND AND BURMA

Burma and Thailand have a historical record of mutual conflict of pre-colonial vintage. During the Second World War, two of the Shan states passed temporarily under Thai control. With the restoration of this territory after the Japanese capitulation, relations between the two countries have been correct rather than cordial. The general introspection of the Ne Win regime in Burma after March 1962 served to reduce inter-state contacts and to sustain this correct relationship.

The relationship became subject to strain, nonetheless, from the late 1960s because of the political activities of the former Prime Minister of Burma, U Nu. Nu was released from detention by the military government in 1966. In April 1969 he succeeded in leaving the country ostensibly to secure medical treatment. However, he immediately launched a campaign to oust Ne Win. Nu and his supporters were granted asylum in Thailand on the conventional condition that they would not engage in political activities. Nu was not restrained by this ordinance but set up a United National Liberation Front to secure his political ends. He claimed, in April 1971, to have united under his leadership elements of the four main groups of ethnic minorities in Burma who have long rejected the authority of the government in Rangoon. Such alleged accomplishments were organized from Thailand where Nu's activities did not appear to have been circumscribed. The dangerous potential for conflict arising out of this situation was recognized by both states during 1973, prompted in part by a common desire to repair diplomatic fences in the wake of the Vietnam agreement. In May Ne Win visited Bangkok and an accord was reached whereby Thailand and Burma committed themselves not to shelter insurgents; also a source of dissension was removed with the departure of U Nu to continue his exile in India. For the time being the potential for conflict has been much reduced.

The conflicts which have been the subject of this chapter draw their force from a number of sources but in the main they reflect reaction and adjustment to transfers of power which have involved a lineal demarcation of states less than familiar to Southeast Asian experience.[9] To some extent they reflect also ideological considerations whose stimulation has tended to come in part from outside the region. The most striking and significant conflict with this ingredient within Southeast Asia has been that between the two states of Vietnam. However, as the fact and force of external intervention in this episode has been so striking, it will be discussed under a different heading in the following chapter.

References

1 See Michael Leifer, 'Peace and War in Cambodia', *Southeast Asia*, Winter–Spring 1971.
2 Modelski, *op. cit.*
3 Frederick P. Bunnell, 'Guided Democracy Foreign Policy', *Indonesia*, October 1966.
4 An excellent interpretive analysis is Donald Hindley, 'Indonesia's Confrontation with Malaysia: A Search for Motives', *Asian Survey*, June 1964. See also Bernard K. Gordon, *The Dimensions of Conflict in Southeast Asia*, New Jersey, 1966; and Arnold C. Brackman, *Southeast Asia's Second Front*, New York, 1966.
5 See in particular, Gordon, *op. cit.*
6 Note the argument in F. B. Weinstein, *Indonesia Abandons Confrontation*, Ithaca, 1969.
7 This section draws on Michael Leifer, *The Philippine Claim to Sabah*, Zug, Switzerland, 1968; and 'The Philippines and Sabah Irredenta', *The World Today*, October 1968.
8 Michael Leifer, 'Astride The Straits of Johore', *Modern Asian Studies*, July 1967.
9 Robert L. Solomons, 'Boundary Concepts and Practices in Southeast Asia', *World Politics*, October 1970.

*Chapter Four*

# REGIONAL CONFLICT AND EXTERNAL
# INTERVENTION

The preceding discussion of intra-regional conflicts has tended, perhaps, to distort a dominating feature of international relations within Southeast Asia, that is the extent to which they have been subject to the influence of outside powers. Although independence removed the sovereign presence of metropolitan countries, this did not mean that the states of the region became the primary determinants of international relations in the region. For example, the United States transferred sovereignty in the Philippines but retained substantial military interests there. Even before the outbreak of the Korean War, its commitment to a policy of containment of Communism in Asia had led the United States to attempt to preserve the political status quo in Indochina. It was the moving spirit in the formation of SEATO and subsequently placed its great material resources at the disposal of the Diem government in Saigon, a political commitment that was to lead to massive military intervention not only in Vietnam but also in the other parts of Indochina.

The extent of financial, diplomatic, and military involvement on the part of the United States in Southeast Asia has not been matched by any other external power. Britain enjoyed the longest tenure before transferring sovereignty but its interests were limited geographically to the Malaysia region despite the formal obligation involved in membership of SEATO. They in no way paralleled the extensive regional concern of the United States. In the wake of confrontation, a reappraisal of the British commitment and presence resulted in a revised and modest form of military involvement in Southeast Asia.

The major involvement of the Communist powers in the region has been in relation to the Democratic Republic of Vietnam which they have supported diplomatically and materially in competition with each other. They have also assumed the role of donor of economic and military aid to favoured non-Communist countries, but the continuity of aid delivery has varied according to the current foreign policy orientation of the country concerned. The sponsorship of revolutionary ideas and movements has involved a more limited allocation of their resources.

Shortly after the end of the Second World War, the Soviet Union, as leader of the world Communist movement, endorsed the practice of revolution as the desirable mode of achieving political goals. But only in the case of Indonesia, was there any direct link between local Communist attempts to seize political power and outside Communist support. Following the post-Korean reversal of attitudes to the 'national bourgeois' leadership of the new states, Soviet and especially Chinese diplomacy became much more open and conciliatory, with the apparent object of winning friends and influencing governments. Subsequently, the interests of the Soviet Union and China diverged and came into conflict. Southeast Asia became then an arena of competition between the two major Communist powers. This competition has been demonstrated strikingly in the case of Vietnam and was displayed also, for a limited period, in Indonesia. In general, the Soviet Union assumed the more conventional diplomatic pose and sought to improve its intergovernmental relationships, while the Chinese assumed the more consistently ideological role and provided vocal encouragement and limited material assistance to assist this end; a role which has been moderated in the aftermath of the Cultural Revolution.

In this chapter, we shall consider the role of external powers in regional conflict. Of all the countries whose policies have had relevance for the states of Southeast Asia, it is the United States which has engaged in the most dramatic and extensive forms of intervention. Its role, therefore, will be considered through specific examples of intervention while that of other external powers will be treated in more general terms.

## The United States

### REGIONAL REBELLION IN INDONESIA

Colonialism was not the sole external influence on Southeast Asia before the transfers of power. The diverse cultures of the region had been shaped throughout two previous millenia by infusions from outside and much of this diversity was sustained during the colonial period to be carried over into independence. The consequent political instability provided opportunities for external powers to intervene to promote the interests of their clients. Such an intervention did occur in Indonesia during the course of an unsuccessful rebellion launched initially in Sumatra in February 1958.

The regional rebellions reflected sectional resentment of the quality of political order in Indonesia and the maldistribution of economic rewards between Java and the outer islands. Effective challenge from the periphery against the centre had begun at the end of 1956 with the rejection of the authority of the central government by local military commanders in Sumatra. The climax to this challenge, stimulated by an increasing turbulence in political life, the expulsion of Dutch residents, and the expropriation of Dutch assets, came in February 1958 when a provisional revolutionary government established itself in West Sumatra and demanded a change in the composition and priorities of the central government. About the same time an allied movement with similar political goals was set up in Sulawesi.[1]

To the Western powers, and to the United States in particular, the apparent decay of the central government and the ability of regional military commanders to deny its authority indicated not only a process of political disintegration but also the prospect of a Communist seizure of power in Jakarta. The dissidents of the outer islands were led by declared anti-Communists who had justified their act of rebellion, in part, because of the increasing prominence in political life of the Indonesian Communist Party. Given this evaluation, it seemed logical for the Western powers to support, or at least reinsure with, the anti-Communist groups which had defied central authority and appeared likely to assume control over major portions of the country. As a consequence, the rebels began to receive material assistance in the form of military supplies through the good offices of agencies of the United States and other Western-aligned governments.[2]

At the official level, there was no attempt to challenge the international status of Indonesia. For example, the American Government did not respond to the rebel demand that the United States Federal Reserve Bank freeze assets held for Indonesia, while American oil companies in Sumatra continued to pay royalties in foreign exchange direct to Jakarta. Nonetheless, the rebels continued to receive a measure of assistance from outside sources even after government military action had virtually crushed the main body of regional resistance in April 1958. Only at the end of 1960 was external assistance withdrawn completely. It has been pointed out that by this time '. . . the United States evidently believed that it had sufficiently strong and reliable allies inside the Indonesian government — particularly the Army under Nasution's leadership — to enable it to dispense with the rebels and that it was merely hurting those allies by the earlier policy of helping to keep the rebellion alive'.[3]

The regional rebellions were a critical event in the internal politics of Indonesia in that they served to assist the establishment of Sukarno's Guided Democracy. Externally, they possessed great significance also. Their failure, especially in the light of outside support, reinforced the orientation which Sukarno was seeking to stamp on the foreign policy of Indonesia, for the experience of the uprisings provided evidence of the insidious nature of the imperialist forces alleged to be encircling the country. The experience also inhibited the United States government in its policies towards Indonesia.

## Intervention in Indochina

In this section, although principal attention will be given to the role of the United States, account will be taken of the involvement of other parties.

### VIETNAM

The Geneva Conference of 1954 halted the conflict between the Viet-Minh and the French and issued proposals for the unification of Vietnam. However, what was assumed by most of the participants at Geneva to be a provisional line of demarcation between zones took on the aspect of a political boundary between states as the government of Ngo Dinh Diem consolidated its internal position with the support of the United States. The effect was to interrupt the struggle for political power throughout Vietnam.

Armed conflict revived in South Vietnam during 1958 and in May 1959 the North Vietnamese leadership took the decision to assume control of the insurrection against the Diem government. By 1960 a major insurgency was under way which received the open support of the Lao Dong Party in September and which in December was organized formally under the sponsorship of the National Liberation Front of South Vietnam, a body which incorporated a Communist leadership revealed in the establishment of the People's Revolutionary Party in 1962. In the early years of the insurgency, the type of Communist support provided was in part diplomatic, but it involved also the introduction south of the seventeenth parallel of trained cadres who had gone north during 1954. The conditions for insurgency, however, were intrinsic to the south and derived in great part from the repressive qualities of the Diem government.

As the conflict within South Vietnam intensified, so the intervening role of the United States became more extensive. Diplomatically, attempts were made to shape the political conduct and priorities of the government in Saigon in order to attract popular support. The evident failure of American efforts to this end was exemplified in the approval and support given by the Kennedy administration to dissident generals in their successful attempt to topple Diem and his regime in November 1963.[4] By this stage, the commitment of the United States to drawing the line against Communist expansion in Southeast Asia had become so entrenched that it was obliged to maintain support for Diem's military successors even when they began to demonstrate even less capacity for good government than their ill-fated predecessor.

American military intervention in the conflict in Vietnam passed through perceptible stages of escalation. At the outset of the Diem administration, American involvement had been confined to financial provision and specialist advice. Military advisers were provided, but up to the end of 1961 their number amounted to less than seven hundred, But in December that year, the late President Kennedy authorized an increase which reached nearly 17,000 by October 1963. Early in 1962 he countenanced the establishment of a military assistance command with an operational as opposed to a purely training function, in addition to the extended provision of military equipment. This qualitative change in the nature of intervention has been described as the equivalent of 'crossing the Rubicon of involvement and escalation'.[5]

The quantitative escalation in force levels authorized by President Kennedy was small compared to that approved by President Johnson during his tenure of office. Such escalation was foreshadowed in August 1964 by aerial bombardment against North Vietnamese oil storage installations and motor-torpedo boats pens, allegedly in retaliation for attacks by North Vietnamese surface vessels against American destroyers on station in the Gulf of Tonkin. This episode was utilized to secure a Congressional resolution which served as a political *carte blanche* for the President in authorizing subsequent acts of military escalation.[6] Following retaliatory raids early in February 1965, in response to an attack on an American barracks in Pleiku in South Vietnam, a regular and intensive aerial bombardment of North Vietnam was begun in March in order to create a negotiable bargaining counter in future diplomacy and also to interdict military supplies moving to the South. Initially, however, the bombing was conceived as an act of retribution, justified by the official American conviction that the war in Vietnam was a direct and sole product of the aggression of the North against the South.

In June 1965, following an official but unadmitted realization that the bombing of the North was having little, if any, impact on the

course of the war in the South, there occurred a progressive introduction of American ground troops entrusted with a combat role.
Their function was to assume the main burden of the war at a
juncture when the South Vietnamese Army was considered to be on
the point of collapse. The consequence of this intervention was a
progressive counter-escalation through the increasing introduction
into the South of North Vietnamese regular military formations.
During this intensive phase of the conflict, which not only saw the
perpetual bombing of North Vietnam but also the infiltration of
sabotage and psychological warfare teams together with commando
raids and shelling from the sea, the continued existence of the
Democratic Republic of Vietnam was not subject to political challenge by the United States. This limitation in the prosecution of war
arose from an evident concern on the part of the United States government to avoid a direct confrontation with the great power allies of
its Communist adversary, in particular the Chinese People's Republic.
And it is believed that direct talks between American and Chinese
diplomats in Warsaw during 1966 produced a tacit and informal
accord on the limits of American military intervention north of the
seventeenth parallel.[7]

The intensification and extension of American involvement in the
war in Vietnam saw the concurrent military intervention of states
allied with the United States in pursuit of its policies in Asia. Thailand, the Philippines, South Korea, Australia, and New Zealand all
sent contingents of both fighting and symbolic kinds in order to
promote a desirable balance of power in Indochina, but also to
demonstrate the value which they placed on their political association with the United States. The large-scale American and allied
military involvement led to conventional military encounters in
which high kill-ratios were claimed, but which produced heavy
American casualties also. The outcome of the process of confrontation was one of stalemate in which parallels were drawn with the
biblical battle between David and Goliath.

This stalemate was broken politically and psychologically with
the dramatic Tet offensive of January 1968 when insurgent and
regular formations launched co-ordinated attacks against principal
urban centres in South Vietnam, including Saigon and Hué, in an
attempt to promote a popular uprising against the government of
President Thieu.[8] This offensive was not a military success in that it
failed to achieve its immediate ends. Also, it involved a costly
expenditure of key cadres. But in the United States, the Tet offensive
had an impact similar to that experienced in France following the
dramatic fall of Dien Bien Phu in 1954. It occurred against a background of growing domestic opposition to the prosecution of the

war and its effect was to point up the unwillingness of American society to sustain the heavy human and material costs involved without corresponding and compensating military success. A direct consequence of the Tet offensive was the decision by President Johnson not to seek re-election and to restrict the extent of the bombing of North Vietnam as a preliminary to negotiations with the North Vietnamese in Paris at the end of 1968.

The Tet offensive and its impact on the political process within the United States led directly to a reappraisal of American policy which expressed itself in the doctrine of military disengagement enunciated by President Nixon in July 1969. This Nixon Doctrine reflected a reappraisal of the efficacy of military intervention by American ground forces in Asia. It reflected also a reassessment of the basis for American intervention in Vietnam which had its intellectual roots in the assumption of power by the Communists in China.

The reappraisal of the official American outlook which began with the enunciation of the Nixon Doctrine in 1969 crystallized with the announcement in July 1971 that the American President would pay a visit to Peking (which took place in February 1972) and culminated in the negotiation of a Vietnam peace settlement in January 1973 which led to a withdrawal of all American forces, if not a cease-fire. One consequence of the prior American emphasis on its vital interest in the outcome of the conflict in Vietnam, underpinned by the scale of its military involvement, had been to convince its allies in Asia of its credibility as patron and protector. However, the agonizing reassessment of priorities expressed in selective military disengagement was to place the reliability of the United States as an ally in Asia in serious doubt. Despite the maintenance of the American policy commitment to the government of South Vietnam and an extensive involvement in air war in Indochina (intensified during 1972), the net effect was to cast doubts on the credibility of the United States and to encourage those Southeast Asian governments concerned, in particular Thailand, to reconsider the value of long-standing alignments.

In the main, opposition to American intervention came from Communist countries and from within the United States. Of the non-aligned states there was limited and muted criticism of the American role, despite the human costs involved. And at the base of such tolerance, whether from Suharto's Indonesia or Ne Win's Burma, was an inclination to contemplate American intervention in terms of countervailing power against the Chinese People's Republic.

The impact of American intervention was to encourage governments in Saigon in their determination to sustain the separate independence of the Republic of Vietnam. Indeed, the greater the visible American commitment, the more recalcitrant any South Vietnamese administration could afford to be in response to initiatives from Washington which appeared to threaten its separate existence. This much was exemplified by Saigon's obstructive response to negotiations with the North Vietnamese and the National Liberation Front in Paris at the end of 1968 and early in 1969 and also at the end of 1972.

## LAOS

As a consequence of the Geneva Conference of 1961–62 Laos was subject to a formal neutralization.[9] Both the United States and North Vietnam agreed to remove all military personnel from the country. The government of Laos became a tripartite coalition with Prince Souvanna Phouma representing the neutral component which he tried to express in his foreign policy. The actual internal political balance was in practice extremely fragile. It rested on the existence of three separate military forces, each with external backing, though this support was to diminish in the case of the neutralists of Kong Lé, who were to come into conflict with the Pathet Lao and divide between right and leftist groupings. Prince Souvanna Phouma sought to paper over this internal political polarization and was sustained in office only through American diplomatic and economic support. The outcome was a so-called rightist-neutralist government without Pathet Lao representation. This breakdown in the formal tripartite structure of government in Vientiane proceeded concurrently with the internationalization of internal conflict.

North Vietnamese contingents are believed to have remained in the eastern uplands of the country, not only to stiffen and instruct Pathet Lao units but also to exercise direct control of the complex of supply routes to South Vietnam, which became of increasing importance as the insurgency intensified in that country. The United States had introduced Special Forces units into Laos before the Geneva Conference. They were replaced in 1963 by civilian clothed advisers, who organized clandestine units composed in the main of Meo hill tribesmen who were used in action against the Pathet Lao zone. In March 1964 tactical air strike operations were mounted by Thai pilots flying American planes. These operations were supported from May by American reconnaisance flights and gradually American pilots flying from bases in Thailand assumed the dominant role. Tactical operations were complemented by saturation bombing from October 1966 and were intensified from March 1968 after the partial halt of bombing in North Vietnam. The purpose of these operations was to weaken the Pathet Lao as an effective fighting force by destroying their social and economic base, as well as to strike against the Ho Chi Minh trail. They were conducted, in the main, with the full knowledge of Prince Souvanna Phouma, whose foreign policy postures did not conceal his dependence on American support and his subordination to the Laotian military in domestic matters.[10]

By 1964 the polarization of internal conflict sustained by external involvement had passed the point of repair by negotiation. Representatives of the three Laotian factions met in Paris in September but were unable to reach any agreement. Laos had become engulfed in the conflict for political power in Vietnam and its government had become a truncated and dependent entity capable only of limited diplomatic initiatives. Its future came to rest on American benefaction and foreign policy became an artificial activity exemplified in the fruitless peregrinations of its Prime Minister in attempts to secure the disengagement of all alien forces.[11] In February 1973, after the Vietnam agreement, an accord was reached whereby a cease-fire would take place and yet another coalition government of national union would be formed between the two opposing internal forces; the pretence of the existence of a neutral third force having been discarded. But, in the absence of the effective implementation of the accord, American bombing of Pathet Lao units has continued, justified by requests from the government in Vientiane.

## CAMBODIA

Cambodia's foreign policy as practised by Prince Sihanouk from the early 1960s was founded on the assumption that the United States was incapable of posing effective countervailing power against the Communists in Indochina. From the onset of the crisis in Laos in 1960 Sihanouk had sought to preserve the political integrity of Cambodia through a policy of assiduous accomodation towards the Chinese and Vietnamese Communists, who publicly acknowledged their respect for the existing boundaries of the state.

As the war in South Vietnam changed in character following the large-scale American military intervention from the middle of 1965 the military priorities of the Vietnamese Communists came increasingly to take precedence over commitments to respect the integrity and neutrality of Cambodia. By early 1969 the revealed extent of Vietnamese Communist use of Cambodian territory for sanctuary purposes became so great that Prince Sihanouk increasingly voiced his resentment of 'Vietcong and North Vietnamese implantations'. The Vietnamese Communist military presence in Cambodia did not

present an imminent threat to the position of Sihanouk's government. Its principal purpose was the attainment of longstanding
goals in South Vietnam and not in Cambodia. Nonetheless, the
willingness of the Vietnamese Communists to go back on public
undertakings produced considerable apprehension about the value of
a placatory policy and led Sihanouk to countenance a continued
American military presence in Southeast Asia.[12]

Prince Sihanouk's deposition in March 1970 brought about a
dramatic transformation in the international position of Cambodia
and also in the extent to which the country was to experience the
violence of military conflict. This transformation arose from the
open challenge to the Vietnamese Communists which was expressed
in a defiant ultimatum by Sihanouk's successors demanding the
withdrawal of their forces within two days. The deposition was
construed as a repudiation of the policy of accommodation to
Communist priorities. It was argued in Hanoi that 'to overthrow
Sihanouk is essentially to oppose his policy of neutrality, peace and
national independence from the Americans'.[13] His political overthrow
was seen to pose a direct threat to Vietnamese Communist interests
and the consequent reaction was to transform an uneasy, if not
unstable, relationship into one of open conflict. Towards the end of
April 1970 there were visible signs of an impending Cambodian
collapse in the face of the Vietnamese Communist attack. At this
juncture the United States government ordered a joint American-
South Vietnamese military intervention into eastern Cambodia
which temporarily disrupted the Vietnamese Communist sanctuary
zone and retrieved the position of the post-Sihanouk government in
Phnom Penh. This intervention brought about a clear polarization
of forces which eliminated the option of non-alignment as a viable
foreign policy for Cambodia. Although in terms of declaratory
policy, the government in Phnom Penh sought to adhere to the
longstanding practice of 'neutrality', the international repercussions
of the deposition of Sihanouk and the consequent external intervention did not permit such continuity. The process of polarization
was reflected in the re-establishment of diplomatic relations by
Cambodia with the governments in Bangkok and South Vietnam
and the close military co-operation with the United States and
South Vietnam, whose forces remained in Cambodia after the
withdrawal of the American contingent at the end of June. At the
beginning of May 1970, the Chinese announced the closure of their
embassy in Phnom Penh and declared that relations with Cambodia
would be conducted henceforth through Prince Sihanouk's Royal
Government of National Union established on 5 May in Peking.
Prince Sihanouk had been resident in the Chinese capital from the

day after his deposition and had established in exile a National United Front (FUNK) which entered into a union with Communist-inspired revolutionary front organizations in Indochina.

Exigency had drawn Cambodia into the fold of an informal alliance and away from the 'neutrality' which was the external hallmark of Sihanouk's rule. A vulnerable military position made it necessary to accept assistance from the United States and South Vietnam and enabled a factious government in Phnom Penh to maintain a precarious existence in a country ravaged by foe and friend. Whereas the Vietnamese Communists treated Cambodia as a springboard for prosecution of military and political goals in South Vietnam, the United States contemplated the erstwhile neutral as a buffer through which to hold off Communist advance, while its dual policy of selective disengagement and Vietnamization in South Vietnam was implemented. The present Cambodian government, faced with the international repercussions of the deposition of Prince Sihanouk, has been obliged to accept the consequences of such a policy and to ponder on the violated and stricken condition of what Prince Sihanouk once described as 'an oasis of peace in Southeast Asia'. And in the absence of a cease-fire and negotiations which might preserve the stake of government in Phnom Penh, American military intervention from the air has continued.

American intervention in Indochina had been prompted by a determination to draw the line against Communist advance. Initially, in South Vietnam and Laos, and subsequently in Cambodia, the United States sought to interpose its military power between client governments and revolutionary forces led by the Vietnamese Communists. Although the application of this power thwarted Communist aspirations, the policy of intervention failed to consolidate the position of America's clients in Indochina. It demonstrated instead the immense difficulties involved in trying to promote political legitimacy at a distance through military means.

## The Chinese People's Republic

China's overall relationship with the countries of Southeast Asia has passed through various stages since the assumption to power of a Communist government in 1949. It has been expressed both in militant disapproval and conciliatory regard. However, a consistent goal running through apparent shifts in policy has been a concern to counter the influence of the United States from a region of great security interest. Following the Geneva settlement of 1954 the government in Peking promoted cordial ties with those states in Southeast Asia willing to maintain an acceptable distance from the United States and Formosa. Notwithstanding certain differences,

Burma, Cambodia, and Indonesia developed working relationships with China. By contrast those countries which opted for membership of the American alliance system in Asia were regarded with scorn and derision in Peking. In general, however, China presented a benign face in Southeast Asia until approximately 1958, when, as a consequence of increasing friction with the Soviet Union, it adopted a more abrasive international policy which reached a peak in the mid-to-late 1960s.

Changes in China's international outlook have contributed to a controversy over Chinese aims within Southeast Asia. In one sense, of course, China is a state-power like any other, with ambitions corresponding to perceptions of interest, tempered in turn by self-assessment of capacity. It is also a country where both a deeply resented experience of humiliation at the hands of the West and the impact of revolution and ideology have strongly influenced attitudes to the outside world. Chinese practice in foreign policy, however, has not been consistent with its declarations which have indicated bombast and semi-hysteria. If one were to point to one quality which has come to characterize Chinese policy towards Southeast Asia, and in particular in reaction to American military intervention in the region, it is caution. This sense of caution exemplified by the Maoist dictum, 'Despise the enemy strategically; take full account of him tactically', may be explained by reference to China's relative shortcomings in military capability. Such caution is congruent also with Chinese revolutionary doctrine.[14]

Its most recent authoritative version is to be found in the statement, 'Long live the victory of People's War', made by the late Marshal Lin Piao in September 1965 in which he asserted *inter alia* that:

In order to make a revolution and to fight a people's war and be victorious, it is imperative to adhere to the policy of self-reliance, rely on the strength of the masses in one's own country and prepare to carry on the fight independently even when all material aid from outside is cut off. If one does not operate by one's own efforts, does not independently ponder and solve the problems of the revolution in one's own country and does not rely on the strength of the masses but leans wholly on foreign aid — even though this be aid from socialist countries which persist in revolution — no victory can be won, or be consolidated even if it is won.

It may be argued that this selected extract from the statment by the now discredited Lin Piao is little more than a rationalization indicating China's unwillingness to countenance a direct confrontation with the United States. This is probably correct, but only in part. There is a certain realism in Chinese revolutionary doctrine which is based on an appreciation of the problems of external intervention, irrespective of the dangers of confronting American military power. Chinese practice in supporting so-called wars of national liberation, however motivated, has been characterized by undoubted limitation. It has not taken the form of direct physical intervention except in two cases, and those do not compare quantitatively with American involvement. In North Vietnam — a close ally — approximately 50,000 Chinese troops have been introduced since 1965 but essentially as a construction corps engaged in rebuilding communication links damaged by American bombing. None of these soldiers is known to have been deployed south of the seventeenth parallel. Chinese engineers have been active also in parts of Northern Laos, building roads whose strategic purpose remains a matter of speculation, even though one spur approaches the Thai border.[15]

In other parts of Southeast Asia, Chinese intervention has taken the form of assistance to revolutionary front organizations, directed usually by a local Communist party. It has involved the provision of material supplies, including weapons, specialized training and other facilities within China, together with propaganda and diplomatic support. Such assistance, especially of the material kind, has been most substantial in the case of the Democratic Republic of Vietnam which has been a long-standing beneficiary. Chinese provision of aid has not always reflected political accord between Peking and Hanoi, especially over the actual conduct of the war south of the seventeenth parallel, which the Chinese felt was becoming unduly conventional from 1965 and likely to provoke an escalating American response. There were significant differences of opinion over the North Vietnamese decision during 1968 to negotiate directly with the Americans in Paris and subsequently over the Chinese willingness, announced in July 1971, to receive President Nixon in Peking. Irrespective of such differences, the Chinese continued to provide material aid for North Vietnam, in part as a product of their competitive relationship with the Soviet Union and also because of a basic interest in assisting the withdrawal of the United States from South Vietnam.

Before the massive military intervention of the United States in Vietnam, the Chinese government supported the goal of a neutral and separate South Vietnam, which suggested a wish to see a loose collection of small conciliatory states on its southern periphery. The scale of American military intervention provoked a change in priorities and a reversal of China's position on the status of South Vietnam. However, China's sponsorship of the Indochinese revolutionary front, which emerged after the overthrow of Prince Sihanouk in March 1970, and the provision of asylum for Prince Sihanouk and his government in exile may be interpreted not only as an initiative to exclude the influence of the Soviet Union from a region regarded as of proprietory interest, but also as a means to forestall the hegemony of Hanoi in Indochina.

Elsewhere in Southeast Asia, China has been less directly involved in support of revolution. Conciliation was long the policy towards the governments of Burma, Cambodia, and Indonesia. In the case of the latter country, China was obliged in 1959 to tolerate discrimination against ethnic Chinese. It has been argued that although it was distasteful to accept Djakarta's discriminatory measures, in so doing Peking once again revealed the extent of her willingness to make concessions in order to protect the possibility of drawing Indonesia into a Chinese-led anti-imperialist coalition.[16] In relations with other non-Communist governments, external policy served as the touchstone for Chinese regard. During the Sukarno period, China provided some material assistance and also vocal diplomatic support, particularly in January 1965 when Indonesia withdrew from the United Nations. Although there were close links with the Indonesian Communist Party (PKI), these were subordinated to the priority of sustaining a close association with a government whose outlook towards the international political system coincided with Chinese interests. A policy of openly advocating the overthrow of the military government of Indonesia was adopted only in July 1967 nearly two years after the abortive coup which led to a political transformation in Indonesia and a consequent change in international orientation.

During the period of the Cultural Revolution, China's relations deteriorated with those Southeast Asian countries which had long been regarded as good friends. This was especially the case in 1967 when Red Guard elements, led by the former chargé d'affaires in Indonesia, Yao Teng-shan, secured temporary control of the Foreign Ministry.[17] The most serious breach occurred in China's relations with Burma. Up to that point, Chinese support for the Burmese Communist Party (White Flag) had not been much more than nominal, while the manner of the settlement and joint demarcation of the Sino-Burmese border was represented as a symbol of harmonious association. In June 1967, however, disturbances took place in Rangoon following attempts by local Chinese students, abetted by officials of the Chinese embassy, to publicize the revolutionary thoughts of Chairman Mao. In the melée, a member of the Chinese embassy staff was killed and this event, plus subsequent demonstrations which could have been inspired only by the

Burmese government, led to a mutual withdrawal of ambassadors and a Chinese call for the overthrow of the Ne Win administration by the Burmese Communist party. Such advocacy made little impact on the political order within Burma. Indeed, the Burmese Communist party proceeded to engage in an exercise in self-decimation as a consequence of personal feuds and doctrinal differences. Concurrently, security operations by government forces destroyed the party's position in the strategic Pegu Yoma heartland of the country. With the phasing down of the Cultural Revolution, especially from 1969, there occurred a process of rapprochement between the Burmese and Chinese governments which was a product of joint initiatives.

Differences arose also between China and Cambodia at the peak of the Cultural Revolution when Prince Sihanouk reacted strongly against what he construed as the obtrusive activities of the Sino-Khmer Friendship Society. In this episode there were not any disturbances to point up the inability of the Chinese government to protect the lives of its officials overseas. At the height of the crisis, Prince Sihanouk threatened to break off diplomatic relations with Peking and in consequence Chou En-lai felt obliged to intervene to repair a relationship that had long been seen to work to China's political advantage. Following the deposition of Prince Sihanouk in March 1970 the Chinese government was cautious in its initial response. It was not until early in May that it transferred recognition to a government of National Union established by Prince Sihanouk in Peking. It is interesting to note that it was not the internal character of the Lon Nol government that antagonized the Chinese, but its refusal to sustain the foreign policy of accommodation to the Vietnamese Communists, which had been the dominant feature of Sihanouk's political practice.[18]

Elsewhere in Southeast Asia, China has pursued a more, if not entirely, consistent policy. China's degree of subversive involvement has tended to depend on the foreign policies pursued by respective Southeast Asian governments. Where such policies have expressed themselves in alignment with the interests of the United States, for example in Thailand. China has adopted a hostile position and has acted to support the aims of revolutionary groups. However, in the actual practice of intervention, and with the exception of Vietnam discussed above, the Chinese contribution to revolutionary movements has been less than substantial.

Peking has served as a centre for Southeast Asian exiles and revolutionary front organizations who have been provided with residential and propaganda facilities. For example, leaders of the Thailand Patriotic Front, which emerged in January 1965, have been fêted at receptions and their statements have been reproduced through the good offices of the New China News Agency. The provinces of southern China harbour clandestine radio stations which transmit to Thailand, Malaysia, the Philippines, and Burma among others in local vernaculars and minority languages. More practical Chinese assistance for revolutionary movements has been affected by the problem of logistics. Thus, its most significant contribution, apart from Vietnam and Laos, would appear to have been made in Thailand, where ease of access through Laos utilizing the facilities of the North Vietnamese and Pathet Lao has enabled the introduction of small arms, propaganda material, and the movement of local cadres to receive specialized training.

Intervention in support of revolutionary movements has been an important aspect of Chinese foreign policy practice in Southeast Asia. But whenever a Southeast Asian state has demonstrated a propensity to pursue a foreign policy which is independent of Western interests, then the public commitment of China to the support of revolution has tended to be tempered — discounting the special circumstances of the Cultural Revolution — by the political advantages of encouraging such a policy. Malaysia represents a recent case in point. Since the succession of Tun Abdul Razak as Prime Minister in September 1970 Malaysia has sought to confirm its position as a self-declared non-aligned state. To this end, its leaders have advocated the neutralization of Southeast Asia under great power guarantee by China, the Soviet Union, and the United States. In consequence — and despite Malaysian participation in the Five Power Commonwealth Force established in 1971 as a substitute for the Anglo-Malaysian Defence Treaty — the Chinese government has become less hostile.

It is difficult to be conclusive on the subject of Peking's determination to promote the spread of Communism in Southeast Asia on the evidence of Chinese revolutionary practice. The evidence that exists suggests a stronger and more consistent concern with foreign policy. Revolutionary practice has been utilized more to mould this aspect of state behaviour than to transform internal political orders. An overriding reality for China in Southeast Asia has been the hostile presence, in one form or another, of the United States. With the exception of policy practice during the period of the Cultural Revolution, the erosion and removal of this presence would appear to have been the principal external goal of China.

The reactions of the states of Southeast Asia to the fact of a Communist China have tended to be dominated by the realities of power. This has not led to equivalent policies, as different states have evaluated their particular situations according to special need.

Thus Burma and Cambodia initially saw little point in antagonizing China by alignment with the United States as long as China did not present a hostile face. Thailand and the Philippines, confident in the resolution of the United States and the capacity of its national power, trusted on countervailing strength against a resurgent China. But, by the outset of the 1970s, attitudes to China began to be reassessed as the United States reappraised its own position in Asia and moved towards a limited détente with Peking.

## The Soviet Union

Geopolitical situation and longstanding priorities in Europe have meant that Southeast Asia has not enjoyed great importance for the Soviet Union. After the Second World War the enunciation of the militant Zhdanov 'two-camp' doctrine at the founding of the Cominform in September 1947 served as a beacon for potential revolutionaries in Southeast Asia. However, the Soviet Union did not provide tangible assistance to Southeast Asian revolutionaries.[19]

Indeed, in 1945 the Soviet government behaved with a cool reserve towards the Viet-Minh after the Japanese capitulation and was much more concerned to advance the political prospects of the French Communist party who supported repressive action against the Viet-Minh as members of the French coalition cabinet until May 1947. Support for Ho Chi Minh's movement came only after the French Communist party left the coalition, but even then the Democratic Republic of Vietnam declared in September 1945 did not receive Soviet recognition until January 1950, after such recognition was offered from the Chinese People's Republic.

At the Geneva Conference on Indochina of 1954 the Soviet Union together with the Chinese exerted pressure on the Viet-Minh to accept a provisional territorial settlement in Vietnam which was a feeble reflection of their military success. At that juncture Soviet priorities had changed. There was no desire to confront the United States. The course of revolution had, by then, foundered abysmally in Burma, Malaya, Indonesia, and the Philippines. An indication of the extent to which the Soviet Union was prepared to accept the post-independence status quo in Southeast Asia was its suggestion, in January 1957, that both North and South Vietnam should be permitted entry into the United Nations together with North and South Korea. Cordial relationships were enjoyed with Cambodia, limited economic assistance went to Burma, while both economic and extensive military assistance was given to Indonesia, especially in 1960–62 as the campaign to secure West Irian intensified. It is difficult, however, to talk of major Soviet intervention. Attempts were made to expand diplomatic influence, but intervention in terms of projection of a physical presence did not take place until 1960.

In August 1960 when Captain Kong Lé mounted a coup in Vientiane in order to change the external orientation of Laos to non-alignment, the Thais inspired a blockade of the Mekong River, to deny essential supplies to the neutralists. It was during this episode that the Soviet Union organized a large-scale airlift of military supplies to stiffen the resistance of the neutralists, then supported by the Pathet Lao and the North Vietnamese. It has been argued that the Soviet Prime Minister Krushchev assumed the risk of intervention in Laos 'to retain the allegiance of North Vietnam in the developing quarrel with China'.[20] Indeed, the initiative of the Soviet Union checked right-wing military dominance in Laos and safeguarded North Vietnamese interests in the eastern uplands of the country.

After the Laotian Conference in 1961–62 Soviet interest in Southeast Asia seemed to wane. Military expenditure in Indonesia did not appear to produce political dividends, given Chinese political encroachments. Nonetheless, the Soviet Union did use its veto power to save Indonesia from political embarrassment when Malaysian charges of aggression were heard before the United Nations Security Council. In Indochina, the Soviet Union was caught by conflicting pressures. On the one hand, it wished to prevent the North Vietnamese from aligning with China, but it was concerned also to urge moderation and negotiation in the interests of its policy of détente with the West, especially after the signature of the partial Nuclear Test Ban Treaty of August 1963. However, after the political demise of Krushchev in October 1964, the Soviet government became more actively committed in support of the policies of North Vietnam. Perhaps the most significant episode which spurred the involvement of the Soviet Union was the commencement of the bombing of North Vietnam by the United States in February 1965 at the very moment that the Soviet Prime Minister Alexei Kosygin was on an official visit to Hanoi, allegedly engaged in advocating a negotiated settlement of the war. With extended American military intervention, the Soviet Union found itself obliged to sustain the military capability of a fellow-Socialist state, especially given the temper of political competition with the Chinese People's Republic.

Elsewhere in Southeast Asia, Soviet involvement was limited. Following the abortive coup in Indonesia in October 1965, the Soviet government had to suffer the indignity of observing the decimation of the Indonesian Communist party by arms which it had supplied to the Indonesian army and for which it had not yet been paid. Subsequently, Soviet practice in Southeast Asia — apart from continued provision of material and diplomatic support for North Vietnam — turned away from ideological concerns towards promoting inter-governmental relations, in part as an aspect of Russia's great power standing, but also in an attempt to contain Chinese political influence. In November 1967 an agreement was reached with the government of Malaysia on the exchange of ambassadors; early in the following year an equivalent accord was reached with the government of Singapore. Striking evidence of Soviet intentions in Asia emerged in June 1969 at an international conference of Communist parties held in Moscow when Party Chairman Leonid Brezhnev remarked: 'We are of the opinion that the course of events is raising the question of creating a system of collective security in Asia'. Such a suggestion did not produce a positive reaction among the states of Southeast Asia. Nonetheless, the Soviet Union has continued with its diplomatic initiatives, for example, cementing economic ties with Malaysia and Singapore and establishing trade and air communications links with Thailand.

In August 1970 the Soviet government agreed to reschedule outstanding Indonesian debts and agreed in principle to revive incompleted aid projects. Attempts were made also at the end of the year to establish formal diplomatic relations with the Philippines. Concurrent with this emphasis on inter-governmental ties, the Soviet government has denounced local Communist parties which have aligned themselves with the Chinese ideological position. For example, in May 1970 the leaders of Communist parties in Burma, Thailand, and Malaysia were accused of having 'blindly followed Mao's instructions, and adopting adventurous Chinese ways'.

An overriding problem for the Soviet Union has, ironically, become that which afflicted the United States in the 1950s and 1960s, namely the containment of the Chinese People's Republic in Asia. To this end, the Soviet Union did not withdraw its diplomatic mission from Phnom Penh, but only reduced its status following the extension of violent conflict from Vietnam to Cambodia and the public commitment of the Chinese for the Sihanouk government in exile in Peking. In its competitive engagement with China, however, the Soviet Union is not a completely free agent as long as the reunification of Vietnam remains the basic priority of the government in Hanoi. It is also likely to experience new forms of competition with China as Peking, once again, begins to deal in Southeast Asia more at the level of governments and less at the level of insurgent movements.

The states of Southeast Asia which are subject to insurgency of one kind or another do not regard the Soviet Union as an external promoter of such enterprises and are moving increasingly to the position of treating it as but another great power with interests which might affect the nature of regional order. In this respect, some states have become apprehensive of the growing naval presence of the Soviet Union in the Indian Ocean. Indonesia and Malaysia, by asserting their joint sovereignty in the Straits of Malacca, have given notice of their opposition to the extension of the conventional military influence of the Soviet Union, even if it is directed to the containment of China.

References

1 An excellent popular account of the uprisings is James Mossman, *Rebels in Paradise: Indonesia's Civil War*, Oxford, 1961.

2 William Stevenson, *Birds' Nests in their Beards*, Boston, 1963.

3 Herbert Feith and Daniel S. Lev, 'The End of the Indonesian Rebellion', *Pacific Affairs*, Spring 1963, p. 41.

4 *The Pentagon Papers*, New York, 1971, pp. 158–233.

5 For a good overall account of American intervention, see G. McT. Kahin and J. W. Lewis, *Vietnam and the United States*, New York, 1969 (revised edition).

6 E. G. Windchy, *Tonkin Gulf*, New York, 1971. Also *Pentagon Papers*, pp. 253–306.

7 *The Times*, London, 1 January 1969.

8 D. Oberdorfer, *Tet*, New York, 1971.

9 George Modelski, *International Conference on the Settlement of the Laotian Question 1961–2*, Canberra, 1962.

10 Useful accounts of American intervention in Laos are to be found in Nina S. Adams and Alfred W. McCoy (eds), *Laos: War and Revolution*, New York, 1960.

11 The most comprehensive and recent account of the condition of Laos is Arthur J. Dommen, *Conflict in Laos: The Politics of Neutralization*, New York, 1971 (revised edition).

12 'Thus, it is permitted to hope that, to defend its world interests (and not indeed for our sake), the United States will not disentangle itself too quickly from our area — in any case not before having established a more coherent policy which will enable our populations to face the Communist drive with some chance of success.' Norodom Sihanouk, 'How Cambodia Fares in the Changing Indonesia Peninsula', *Pacific Community*, April 1970, pp. 351–2.

13 *Vietnam Courier*, Hanoi, 23 November 1970.

14 For a good general account of the theory and practice of Chinese foreign policy see P. Van Ness, *Revolution and Chinese Foreign Policy*, California, 1970.

15 See the map of the Chinese roads in Dommen, *op. cit.*, p. 285. The Thai government has claimed that 200 Chinese troops of Meo origin have been supporting insurgents in Thailand since late 1971.

16 David Mozingo, 'China's Policy towards Indonesia', Tang Tsou (ed.), *China's Policies in Asia and America's Alternatives*, Chicago, 1968, p. 336. For China's policy towards the overseas Chinese see Stephen FitzGerald, *China and the Overseas Chinese*, Cambridge, 1972.

17 Melvin Gurtov, *The Foreign Ministry and Foreign Affairs in China's Cultural Revolution*, Rand Corporation Memorandum, Santa Monica, March 1969.

18 J. S. Grant, L. A. G. Moss and J. Unger (eds), *Cambodia: The Widening War in Indochina*, New York, 1971, p. 111.

19 An excellent account of Soviet policies towards Southeast Asia up to the death of Stalin is provided in Charles B. McLane, *Soviet Strategies in Southeast Asia*, New Jersey, 1966.

20 Dommen, *op. cit.*, p. 179.

*Chapter Five*

# CHANGING PRACTICE IN FOREIGN POLICY

More than a quarter of a century after the end of the Second World War and the onset of decolonization, Southeast Asia is still affected strongly by the policies of external powers. Although such powers have not necessarily been able to determine the course of events within the region, any change of direction by them, even if prompted by failure as in the case of the United States in Indochina, has an important bearing on international relations within the region. Thus, the reappraisal of American interests revealed in the enunciation and application of the Nixon Doctrine and, to a much lesser extent, in the drastic reduction by Britain of its military presence, has pointed to a new but, as yet, undefined power balance in which other external powers, notably China and Japan, could play a more important role. This uncertain prospect has become a critical factor in influencing the approach to foreign policy at the outset of the 1970s, especially on the part of those states which have relied heavily in the past on external support.

With this changing situation in mind, we shall examine the most recent phase in the foreign relations of the new states, after first taking note of a trend within the region which emerged during the 1960s.

## The Record of Regional Association
Intra-regional co-operation and schemes for more far-reaching integration have long been mooted for Southeast Asia. Early endeavours in economic co-operation took place within the wider framework of the United Nations Economic Commission for Asia and the Far East, which was established in 1947. By the beginning of the 1970s this organization included every Southeast Asian state

with the exception of North Vietnam. ECAFE has functioned primarily to promote multilateral collaboration in the collection and exchange of economic data, the establishment of uniform standards and in the planning stages of development programmes. One notable exception to this advisory role has been the promotion of a scheme to control and develop the use of the waters of the Mekong River which flow through Thailand, Laos, Cambodia, and South Vietnam.[1] The funds for the scheme have been channelled through ECAFE and the planning of the enterprise, now interrupted in part by the course of war in Indochina, has involved the active co-operation of all the riparian states even when diplomatic relations have been broken between some of them.

In 1951 the Colombo Plan was set up to serve members of the Commonwealth in Asia and subsequently extended its membership. It has functioned as a means of putting prospective aid donors and recipients into effective communication with each other. More recent developments in economic association include the Asian Development Bank, set up in Manila in 1966, which functions on strict banking principles, and recurrent intra-regional ministerial conferences which are used, in the main, as ways of channelling Japanese economic assistance.

Intra-regional economic association has lagged within Southeast Asia because its basis is so limited. The various economies are based in the main on the production and export of primary goods and as such do not stand in complementary relationship to each other. Indeed the countries of the region offer each other much less than can be gained through bilateral ties with external powers, especially Japan. Extra-regional trade is currently increasing more rapidly than intra-regional commerce.

Greater, if still modest, achievement has taken place in political association. Early efforts in this direction had foundered either because of conflicting state interests or because they were externally inspired. In Southeast Asia proper, there was an absence of positive measures for institutional association until 1961. In July that year, the governments of Malaya, the Philippines, and Thailand set up between them the Association of Southeast Asia (ASA).[2] In an attempt to attract the non-aligned countries of the region, its aims were limited to social and economic co-operation. It failed to demonstrate any potential for growth, however, and foundered on the Sabah claim and confrontation. At one juncture during the initial months of confrontation, the tripartite diplomacy between Malaya, Indonesia, and the Philippines produced a plan for closer association of these three states of Malay origin called Maphilindo. In essence, this was a diplomatic device designed to deal with the conflict over the desirability of Malaysia. But it too expired in the acrimony which succeeded the establishment of Malaysia in September 1963.

A fresh climate for a new and practical initiative in regional association was created following the abortive coup attempt in Indonesia of 1 October 1965 and the consequent end of confrontation. One motive for the promotion of a new institutional expression of regional association was a conviction by countries like Thailand and Malaysia that it was necessary to provide some recognition of the regional standing of Indonesia and, at the same time, to contain any propensities on its part for a hegemonial position. In August 1967, one year after the formal termination of confrontation, the foreign ministers of Indonesia, Malaysia, Thailand, the Philippines, and Singapore met together in Bangkok to set up the Association of Southeast Asian Nations (ASEAN). This body was, in effect, to supersede ASA whose members came together only once more under its auspices. Since its formation, ASEAN has experienced a modest progress and some internal difficulties. The progress has taken the form of attempts to harmonize policies and economic activities rather than schemes for substantial regional co-operation. Ministerial meetings have taken place regularly in the respective capitals of the member states, but their scope has been restricted and a common theme and understanding has been the need to proceed with care and caution, especially in any consideration of a security function for ASEAN. Nevertheless, the Association has achieved something more than just mere existence and has survived conflicts among its members, in particular the acrimonious exchanges between the Philippines and Malaysia which revived during 1968 to cause a temporary rupture in diplomatic ties.

ASEAN is less a demonstration of great practical achievement than an indication of a measure of common interests, particularly about the relationship between intra-regional accord and internal political order. Unlike preceding bodies, it has not become a source of controversy in the region and both the United States and the Soviet Union regard it with differing toleration. ASEAN does not display any active hostility to China. Indeed, in the light of American and British disengagement from the region, a prime object is to secure Chinese recognition of the legitimate role of ASEAN as the appropriate concert for resolving intra-regional problems.

*Foreign Policy in the 1970s*
The practice of foreign policy within Southeast Asia has been confined to élite circles with only limited reference to popular response.[3] Where popular response has played a role in the foreign policy process it has usually been the product of governmental initiatives which

seek to utilize foreign policy for domestic political purpose. The most striking example of such conduct occurred in Indonesia during the Sukarno era, but it has taken place elsewhere. Burma in June 1967 when the government inspired anti-Chinese demonstrations, and Cambodia during and after Sihanouk's rule, when external antagonisms were utilized to promote internal solidarity, provide some additional examples.

This élite monopoly of foreign policy has not changed in essence in the period under discussion. What has changed however, under the impact of events discussed above, has been the perception by foreign policy makers of their international environment. It is now less realistic to label states neatly as aligned or non-aligned.

## Burma

Under the military government of Ne Win, Burma has led a somewhat cloistered international existence. The Burmese government's assessment of its national priorities has promoted the conviction that limitations on external contact will reduce the prospect of conflict and permit maximum attention to internal needs. Burma's principal external security concern has long focused on the Chinese People's Republic and it has been policy to avoid initiatives which might provoke the wrath of Peking. Such a policy, however, has not been practised at the expense of Burmese interests. Burma, although willing to be conciliatory, has sought to avoid the role of obsequious supplicant.

An example of this was the crisis of June 1967 when Rangoon experienced minor manifestations of the Cultural Revolution among the local Chinese community. The Burmese government made its point in an abrasive manner and in the autumn of that year began to receive limited military aid from the United States. Subsequently it sought to mend fences and establish a more cordial association with China. In March 1971 a Chinese ambassador once again took up residence in Rangoon. This initiative did not make for a restoration of a prior relationship, but the establishment of a more correct one. Indeed, at the end of that month, a radio transmitting station describing itself as the *Voice of the People of Burma* began operating in South China. In August 1971, however, Ne Win paid a visit to China and on his return indicated that the normalization of relations had progressed considerably.

Past strain in the relationship with China did not result, however, in any dramatic reordering of priorities in foreign policy. A recognition of the limited utility of alternative options dictated by geopolitical circumstances has prevented any disposition to alignment. Thus, the United States has not been encouraged to contemplate a close association. A limited amount of economic assistance plus some unpublicized military aid has been provided, but the American presence in Burma is inconspicuous. Relations are somewhat closer with the Soviet Union, also a modest benefactor, which is pleased to represent Burma as a model among and for developing countries, not only because of the distance which it keeps from the United States but also, and more importantly, because Burma has sought to demonstrate its independence from the influence of China.

Regionally, within Southeast Asia, Burma plays a limited role and has not been an active opponent of the war in Vietnam. It is also not a vocal public advocate of non-alignment although such a policy is represented as a constituent element of 'The Burmese Way to Socialism'. Relations with the members of ASEAN are, in general, much more than just correct, but there has not been any indication of a desire to join the organization even though Ne Win has paid lip service to the Malaysian proposal for the neutralization of Southeast Asia.

*Thailand*

If Burma has demonstrated over time a strong measure of consistency in the practice of foreign policy, Thailand has moved towards a more equivocal international position. Uncertainty over policy alternatives had existed from the early 1960s, when the American response to the situation in Laos gave concern in Bangkok. Constant reassurance was necessary to assuage such concern, exemplified by the Dean Rusk–Thanat Khoman joint communique of March 1962 in which the United States indicated that its obligation to defend Thailand did not depend upon the prior agreement of the other members of SEATO.

The massive American military intervention in Vietnam during 1965 served to reassure the Thai government that the political will of its ally and patron was not subject to doubt. Thailand had become involved in American intervention as what were nominally sovereign Thai bases were used in aerial bombardment in Indochina. The Thai commitment to this undertaking was not without some reservation, however. The prospect of retaliation moved the Thais to seek and secure during 1965 a secret agreement with the United States which provided for protection in the case of a direct external threat.[4]

Thai involvement in the American military enterprise in Indochina continued through the late 1960s. In May 1967 a first contingent of 2,500 combat troops was despatched to South Vietnam and another of 10,000 in the following May. However, at the first significant sign of a weakening in American resolve, the Thais began to reconsider their international position. Thus, there was considerable anxiety following the decision by President Johnson in March 1968 to restrict the extent of the bombing in North Vietnam in an attempt to initiate negotiations. The commencement of the Vietnam peace talks in Paris also produced a Thai response. In February 1969 Foreign Minister Thanat Khoman announced that once hostilities were terminated in Vietnam, American troops would have to leave Thailand. He spoke out also against the corrupting influence on Thai society of the American military presence.

The Thai government's concern at the consequences of alignment with an irresolute United States became much more acute following the enunciation of what became known as the Nixon Doctrine. In the light of the American desire for military disengagement it was no coincidence that early in October 1970 a North Vietnamese delegation arrived in Bangkok to resume talks suspended during 1964 on the repatriation of the approximately 40,000 Vietnamese living in the northeast of Thailand. The revival of these negotiations, which were almost certainly concerned with matters other than repatriation, indicated that Thailand might be willing to seek some form of understanding with Asian Communist states as an alternative to a defiant anti-Communism based on secure alignment with the United States. In the same year, Thanat Khoman disclosed that he had sought to initiate a diplomatic dialogue with the Chinese People's Republic.

By 1971 the Thai government appreciated fully that the impact of the course and conduct of the war in Vietnam on the American public and on Congressional attitudes meant that much certainty had gone out of the relationship between Bangkok and Washington. Indeed, in March 1971 Thanat Khoman announced that 'while Thailand is willing to continue sincere relationships and co-operation with nations of the West, it entertains little, if any, illusion about the reliability and consistence of response from the latter'. President Nixon's visit to Peking in February 1972 served only to underline such a sentiment.

Shortly before this visit, however, the early prospect of a new course in Thai foreign policy was rendered less likely. On 17 November Prime Minister Thanom Kittikachorn suspended the parliamentary constitution and declared martial law. This return to total military rule was precipitated by legislative obstructionism, but was a reaction also to domestic response to the entry of China into the United Nations. By this action, the Thai Prime Minister reasserted control of foreign policy, without giving it a new sense of direction. Although Thailand entered into 'ping-pong' diplomacy and sent a team to participate in the Asian table-tennis championships in Peking in August 1972, it also willingly provided additional bases for the United States when it revived the bombing of North Vietnam from the spring of that year. Thus, old options, even if uncertain, have been retained while new ones are being explored.

*Laos and Cambodia*
Laos, torn still by the force of internal dissension and external intervention despite a formal cease-fire agreement in February 1973, experiences a fragmented existence and an artificial international status. Its government remains a perpetual debtor and relies heavily on the United States and its allies for budgetary support. The consistent aim of Prime Minister Souvanna Phouma has been to secure an integral and united Laos free of foreign domination. However, the ramifications of war in Vietnam have been such as to subordinate Laos to the priorities of outside powers.

Cambodia has come to experience a condition similar to that of Laos. With a feeble military and economic capacity and a broken provincial administrative apparatus, Cambodia is also greatly dependent on the economic benefaction of the United States and the air support facilities which it supplies. In such circumstances the practice of foreign policy is directed to the continued provision of such allied support, which is vital for survival of the Lon Nol government. In the event of a total military disengagement of the United States from the mainland of Asia, Cambodia could well undergo a traditional experience, whereby a dissident prince is restored by an external patron power but rules as its client.

*The Republic of (South) Vietnam*
Foreign policy for South Vietnam is linked closely to the prosecution of a war whose outcome will determine the political identity of the truncated state. In this endeavour the government of President Thieu is concerned, above all, to sustain its special relationship with the United States. A willingness to lend support, if not conviction, to the philosophy of the Nixon Doctrine has been necessary to ensure a constant and vital supply of material and military assistance from the United States, which enables the Saigon government to resist the political demands of its Communist adversaries irrespective of any obligations undertaken in the Vietnam Settlement of January 1973.

Within Southeast Asia, South Vietnam enjoys only limited relationships. Ties have been closest with the Philippines and Thailand and, since May 1970, with Cambodia, although there is considerable tension in that association. Because of its questionable position and legitimacy, South Vietnam was not included in early initiatives in regional association. But with the formation of ASEAN, incorporating a formally non-aligned but unequivocally anti-

Communist Indonesia, South Vietnamese representatives with observer status have participated in ministerial meetings of the association.

## The Democratic Republic of (North) Vietnam

Like South Vietnam, the state to the north of the seventeenth parallel has a vital interest in the outcome of a conflict seen, in its case, as a struggle for reunification. To this end and through military necessity, North Vietnamese forces have operated not only in South Vietnam but also in Laos and Cambodia. Foreign relations for North Vietnam have involved above all, the management of a dual association with the Soviet Union and the Chinese People's Republic. These two countries represent the major source of external military and material assistance for the prosecution of war. However, because of the sustained animosity between the external Communist powers, North Vietnam is obliged to be circumspect about the manner in which it responds to competitive political wooing. It has managed with great skill to retain a considerable degree of independence within the triangular relationship, although concern has been expressed at the onset of détente between the Chinese People's Republic and the United States.

Aside from this key relationship, which could change with modifications in great power policies, foreign relations take place at a less conventional level. North Vietnam has played a prominent role in sponsoring revolutionary movements in Indochina as a whole and not solely in South Vietnam. In April 1970, following the over-throw and exile of Prince Sihanouk, the North Vietnamese assumed a prominent part in a 'Summit Conference of Indochinese Peoples' held somewhere in southern China.[5] The North Vietnamese have made it a point to secure the support of peoples as well as govern-ments for what they represent as a legitimate cause. In this endeavour constant contacts are maintained with radical and sympathetic groups in the Western world who have been active in pressing their governments either to denounce or to withdraw support from American policies in Southeast Asia.

## Malaysia

The termination of confrontation, the emergence of a friendly government in Jakarta and a major adjustment in Britain's military role in Southeast Asia have encouraged an increasingly independent outlook in foreign policy by Malaysia. This orientation was given additional emphasis with the departure from office of Tunku Abdul Rahman in September 1970 and the succession as prime minister of Tun Abdul Razak. Although the Tunku had been a pioneer in the promotion of regional association within Southeast Asia, his outlook and idiom reflected considerable attachment to Commonwealth ties and especially to Britain — perceived as the cornerstone of foreign and defence policy. The experience of confrontation vindicated this outlook, but in its aftermath a resentment of an underlying paternalism, together with a suspicion of British partiality for the independent Singapore of Lee Kuan Yew, stimulated a reappraisal of international position by influential officials within the Ministry of Foreign Affairs.

Given a benevolent and co-operative Indonesia, security has come to be viewed essentially as an internal problem, even though Communist insurgency is encouraged from outside the country. Such a view of security in conjunction with the prospect of a new Asian power balance prompted an official commitment to a policy of neutralization for the entire region of Southeast Asia, guaranteed through great power accord.[6] It has encouraged also a willingness to contemplate a dialogue with the Chinese People's Republic, which bore fruit during 1971.

In part response to the example of Indonesia, Malaysia has espoused a moderate non-alignment. In his first speech following his assumption of the office of prime minister, Tun Razak stressed the independent course of his country's foreign policy and made no mention of Malaysia's Commonwealth attachments or the five-power Commonwealth force which was to replace the military arrangements of the Anglo-Malaysian Defence Agreement. But underlying Malaysia's non-aligned posture is a cautious pragmatism and a vigorous internal policy of anti-Communism. At the Conference of Non-Aligned States held in Guyana in August 1972 the Malaysian delegation (with those of Indonesia and Laos) walked out in protest at the seating of representatives from the Provisional Revolutionary Government of South Vietnam.

## Singapore

Singapore began its independent existence with an acute sense of vulnerability and a fear of being overcome through the joint hostility of Indonesia and Malaysia. The choice of military advisers from Israel to assist in building up an army almost from scratch pointed up the analogy of Singapore as the Israel of Southeast Asia, set uncomfortably in a hostile Muslim sea. And indeed, in its attitude to its near neighbours, Singapore has tended to display, from time to time, an abrasiveness in its foreign relations characteristic of Israeli postures.

An underlying pragmatism, however, has served to moderate a natural propensity on the part of Singapore for persistent public acrimony in relations with Malaysia. For example, it is recognized that the racial problems of the peninsula cannot be isolated from the island-state. In addition, there is an understanding that the geopolitical situation and the requirements of aerial defence demand bilateral co-operation across the Straits of Johore within the context of the five-power Commonwealth force set up in November 1971.

In the realm of foreign policy, however, there remains a marked difference between Singapore and Malaysia. Whereas Malaysia, which has proposed the neutralization of Southeast Asia, predicates its policy on a benevolent Indonesia, Singapore looks to its south with much more suspicion. Singapore's perception of security derives in part from its minute size and vulnerable position, and also from its regional identity as a predominantly Chinese city-state in a part of the world where Chinese have long been resented and suspect. Although the government of Singapore has sought to present a multiracial aspect through its domestic policies, it is unable to provide the prism through which neighbouring countries view the island-state.

This fact has governed Singapore's international outlook, indicated by its Foreign Minister Rajaratnam in May 1970 when he asserted: 'It is necessary particularly for the smaller powers in Asia to realize this fact about the big powers. They cannot escape the gravitational pull of great powers but they can, by intelligent calculation about the right distances and the correct velocity, orbit without being destroyed and even with profit to themselves'. Underpinning this hypothesis is a conviction which expressed itself before the Malaysian interest in neutralization and which places a different interpretation on that concept. Singapore, with a strong political base but a vulnerable international position, envisages both stability and advantage in encouraging an ordered involvement of external forces which will neutralize themselves and any threat posed by a dominant regional power.

## Indonesia

The foreign policy of Indonesia under the 'New Order' of President Suharto has been modest and restrained. As a consequence of this change in international position, the United States and its allies reconsidered their previously negative attitude towards a revival of foreign aid and investment and subsequently agreed to reschedule outstanding external debts over a thirty year period on highly favourable terms. An additional indication of the new direction of Indonesian foreign policy was an involvement with recent antagonists in regional association.

The evident transformation of the style and practice of Indonesian foreign policy has not involved, however, any disregard of important interests or Indonesia's long-standing aspiration to play a major role in influencing the nature of regional order. But by contrast with the Sukarno period, it is recognized that to achieve such a position bellicose conduct must be eschewed and a sound economic base must be established. President Suharto was explicit in this latter respect when he remarked during 1969: 'The matter is that we shall only be able to play an effective role if we ourselves are possessed of a great national vitality'.[7]

The government of Indonesia, like that of Malaysia, considers the problem of security primarily in terms of subversion and insurgency posing a threat to the fabric of the state. The source of challenge is represented in terms of Communist sponsorship and direction and such portrayal has some plausibility in East and Central Java and along the northern border of Kalimantan. The question of security is perceived also in a regional context whereby a process of political erosion within Southeast Asia could culminate in the establishment of springboards for the promotion of insurgency. Thus, Cambodia has been regarded as the weak underbelly of Southeast Asia. In May 1970 Indonesia sponsored, without success, a diplomatic gathering to secure a political solution to the conflict which enveloped that country after the fall of Sihanouk. Closer to its shores, the Indonesian government has indicated concern lest the Malaysians mishandle their racial problems to permit communal embroilment to work to Communist advantage. It is worthy of note that the Indonesian government quietly approved the decision by the British government during 1970 to retain a modest military presence in Southeast Asia within the wider framework of a five-power Commonwealth force. It also maintains close bilateral ties with Australia and New Zealand.

Indonesia's interest in regional order has been expressed in its membership of ASEAN. It appears a matter of some conviction that if the five members of the association are able to co-operate together in functional endeavours and in the harmonization of external policies then national energies will be channelled to promote internal stability. Such an outcome is seen as one practical means of sheltering Indonesia and its neighbours from subversion and insurgency. Secondly, ASEAN is envisaged as the vehicle through which a willing acceptance of Indonesia's political primacy — as opposed to hegemony — may be facilitated within Southeast Asia.

Indonesia has demonstrated anxiety about the consequences of a changing power balance in Asia, in particular because of an acute consciousness of current military weakness. This factor, among others, has inhibited a normalization of relations with China (interrupted in October 1967) which Indonesia would like to treat with as an equal and not as a supplicant. Although Indonesia has welcomed, in principle, the Malaysian proposal for the neutralization of Southeast Asia, it retains strong reserve about it as a vehicle for a rapprochement with China. Indeed, Indonesia is keen to demonstrate that it is capable of filling any power vacuum without the involvement of external powers. And it has indicated its sense of proprietary rights towards external powers, especially Japan and the Soviet Union, in declaring jointly with Malaysia that the Straits of Malacca are no longer an international waterway.

### The Philippines

After a phase during the 1960s when a search for a revitalized Asian identity found expression in foreign policy, the Philippines has come to lose a sense of clear direction. Regional association is now an orthodoxy to which only lip service is paid, and as a lesser power within ASEAN, which offers little domestic dividend to President Marcos, the Philippines has not been distinguished by the quality of its commitment to that body.

External threats to security have no real immediacy. Of more significance for the future decade has been the revival of insurgency in Central Luzon, with a so-called New People's Army enjoying regular propaganda support from Radio Peking. Also, in the Muslim south of the country, unrest provoked by administrative and economic neglect, together with sharp practice in land allocation, has manifested itself in armed rebellion. The presidency of Ferdinand Marcos has not brought a significant improvement in economic welfare. And faced with increasing youthful and other political dissent (to which he reacted in authoritarian manner in September 1972), foreign policy has received only limited priority, with the exception of the relationship with the United States.

This relationship is distinguished by its love-hate feelings because of its inherent inequality. For example, the Philippines disengaged its forces from Vietnam, despatched there on American insistence, after a resentful public discovered that they had been used as mercenaries. Nonetheless, a sense of dependence and traditional attitudes to foreign policy have led only to a somewhat artificial debate on the appropriate course to follow as the United States demonstrates decreasing need of the Philippine connection. A fundamental problem which now faces the Philippines is how to renegotiate agreements with the United States which have been economically beneficial but psychologically uncomfortable. Unfortunately, the heady style of Philippine foreign policy practice does not necessarily make for cool and prudent calculation of national interests.

The individual foreign policies which we have considered reflect, above all, the diversity which Southeast Asia exemplifies in almost every respect. In the concluding chapter, we shall try to place these foreign policies in both regional and global perspective.

References

1 W. R. Derrick Sewell, 'The Mekong Scheme: Guideline for a Solution to Strife in Southeast Asia', and David Jenkins, 'The Lower Mekong Scheme' in *Asian Survey*, June 1968.

2 For some information on the formation of ASA see Bernard K. Gordon, *Dimensions of conflict in Southeast Asia*, New Jersey, 1966, pp. 165–172.

3 Werner Levi, *The Challenge of World Politics in South and Southeast Asia*, New Jersey, 1968, Ch. I.

4 A. Casella, 'U.S.–Thai Relations', *The World Today*, March 1970.

5 *Signal Victory of the Militant Victory of the Three Indochinese Peoples*, Hanoi, 1970.

6 M. Ghazalie bin Shafie, 'Neutralization of Southeast Asia', *Pacific Community*, October 1971.

7 President Suharto, 'The State of the Nation', *The Indonesian Review of International Affairs*, July 1970, p. 21.

*Chapter Six*

# TOWARDS A REGIONAL ORDER?

Although some states of Southeast Asia have known independence for over a quarter of a century, constraints imposed by size and persisting political and economic weakness have meant that they occupy a position in the global international system which compares with the experience of the region before the advent of colonial domination. This position of subordination is exemplified individually in the case of Indonesia which stands out as an exception in Southeast Asia in terms of geographic scale and population. It has not been an exception, however, to the general experience of the region in facing acute problems of internal political order which have threatened its national integrity.

Individually and collectively, the states of Southeast Asia have had only an indirect impact outside of their regional locale. When they have extruded, it has been primarily as a consequence of the competitive interest and intervention of external powers. And great diplomatic occasions concerned with Southeast Asia have served, in the main, to demonstrate the full extent of external power involvement in support of regional clients. In addition, within the region, the constituent states have been unable to act effectively in concert to try and shape the pattern of regional order. The achievement of institutional expression to that end has been meagre indeed, and divergent interests and mutual antagonisms have made a common approach, to try and compensate in some small way for a long-standing global subordination, impossible to attain.

An overriding feature of Southeast Asia is that the diversity which constitutes the striking characteristic of its human dimension finds expression also in international relations. At the outset of decolonization and well into the 1950s, foreign policy tended to be based on two alternative approaches to security. These dual approaches derived from divergent assessments of national weakness and the utility of alignment in a bi-polar world. By the 1970s, that bi-polar world had become transformed, though not out of recognition, but the political condition of the states of Southeast Asia had endured with greater consistency while the need to take account of and adjust to the play of external forces had become no less evident or important.

The major external factors which have been engaging the attention of the regional states are the reappraisal of American policy in Asia, the prospect in consequence of a more influential China and the attempt, in turn, by the Soviet Union to counter the extension of such influence. In addition, there is the large-scale and ubiquitous economic involvement of Japan, a country which has been affected equally by the above changes and whose military potential is viewed with apprehension by states for whom the Pacific War was an agonizing experience. In this context of a changing power balance, fraught with uncertainty in advance of any final settlement in Indochina, the practice of foreign relations points up the differences between those states in Southeast Asia capable and those incapable of taking any initiative bearing on the nature of future regional order.

For almost all the states of the region, foreign policy is essentially a reactive process and, for some, it is virtually a meaningless one. For example, in Indochina, South Vietnam has survived by grace of the awesome firepower of the United States and with the military withdrawal of its patron has an uncertain future as an independent entity. Loas and Cambodia, for their part, experience a condition of total dependence and total vulnerability and can only wait on events. In a different context and with a different conception of threat, Burma shows little sign of radically altering its monastic approach to international life even though it has come to exhibit concerns other than sustaining a viable relationship with China. For a vulnerable state, like Thailand, most exposed to the consequences of Vietnamese Communist success in Indochina, foreign policy has become a matter of trying to manage contrasting bilateral relationships. It retains access to a questionable counterveiling power provided by the United States, while gingerly exploring the prospect of a *modus vivendi* with China which might possibly serve to contain the influence of the Vietnamese Communists in a manner pioneered first by Prince Sihanouk.

Of all the states of Southeast Asia, a major initiative on a regional scale has come only from Malaysia which, by contrast with its northern neighbour, does not face any immediate external security problems. In an attempt to transform the basis of regional order, the government of Tun Razak has advanced a proposal for the neutralization of Southeast Asia described as a means to prevent the predominance of any one external power and to remove external power rivalries altogether. This proposal secured only a qualified approval at a meeting of ASEAN foreign ministers held in Kuala Lumpur in November 1971, in the aftermath of the entry of the Chinese People's Republic into the United Nations. Neutralization has been attempted in Southeast Asia only once before, and without success, in the case of one country, namely, Laos. For such a scheme to work effectively, irrespective of the scale on which it is applied, there has to be an identity of interests between both internal and external parties to the agreement. So far, the Malaysian proposal has not been the subject of discussion among the external powers, and there is no reason to expect that it could be, in advance of any stable settlement in Indochina or in the current climate of Sino-Soviet relations. Within the region, the proposal has been discussed within the forum of ASEAN but was supported only in terms of a determination 'to secure the recognition of, and respect for, Southeast Asia as a zone of peace, freedom, and neutrality' which would appear to indicate a somewhat different set of concepts from that of neutralization.

Within the context of ASEAN, the initiative of Malaysia lost force because of the undoubted reserve of Indonesia which regarded the very idea of neutralization guaranteed by external powers as demeaning. Indonesia has been supported in its opposition by Singapore and indirectly by the Philippines whose President's interest in the scheme was motivated by a desire to hold an Asian summit conference in Manila. Subsequently, in August 1972 the Deputy Prime Minister of Thailand, General Praphas, breached the formal solidarity of ASEAN when he announced that Thailand could not be a neutralized country because it was still facing aggression from the Communists.

The Malaysian initiative has foundered, in effect, on the veto of Indonesia, the most important country within ASEAN and one whose friendship is the cornerstone of foreign policy in Kuala Lumpur. The differing but negative reactions of the ASEAN states is a striking example of the immense difficulty involved in securing a common approach to regional order within Southeast Asia. Malaysia, which is a small country with a sizeable overseas Chinese community, sees profit from an arrangement which can attract the approval of China. But Indonesia, its closest associate, regards the neutralization scheme as unduly constricting and also likely to deny a status within the region which it needs time to establish. It would prefer to see as an alternative the development of ASEAN as a consultative vehicle which, through an improved and effective functioning, would itself determine the basis for regional order with

Indonesian leadership and without external participation. This optimistic assumption is barely plausible, however, given the joint resources of the ASEAN states, and their evident divergent interests which have impeded the progress of regional co-operation although there is a growing common recognition of the need to take account of North Vietnam (and possibly a united Vietnam dominant in Indochina) as a major factor in international relations within Southeast Asia.

A regional order, or the prospect for stability in Southeast Asia, which is an elusive and subjective notion, will depend in part on a willingness among the major external powers to tolerate and help sustain a post-war settlement in Indochina. But such a willingness will rest, in turn, on the internal political condition of the states of the region. Difficulties in preserving a *modus vivendi* between external powers are most likely to arise if internal political change or its prospect undermines the basis for any multilateral stand-off. Within Southeast Asia, however, the prognosis for internal political order is uncertain. In consequence, the self-constraint of competing external powers cannot be assumed where they have a special interest in domestic political succession. This means that, for the time being, the major contribution that the new states of Southeast Asia can make to a regional order will be to show themselves capable of overcoming an internal debility which has been their striking common characteristic since independence.

# BIBLIOGRAPHY

*General*
LEVI, WERNER. *The Challenge of World Politics in South and Southeast Asia*, Prentice-Hall, 1968.
GORDON, BERNARD K. *The Dimensions of Conflict in Southeast Asia*, Prentice-Hall, 1966.
LYON, PETER. *War and Peace in South-East Asia*, Oxford University Press, 1969.
JANSEN, G. H. *Afro-Asia and Non-Alignment*, Faber & Faber, 1966.
LAMB, ALISTAIR. *Asian Frontiers: Studies in a Continuing Problem*, Praeger, 1968.

*Burma*
JOHNSTONE, W. C. *Burma's Foreign Policy*, Harvard University Press, 1963.
Burma Socialist Programme Party. *Foreign Policy of the Government of the Union of Burma*, Rangoon, 1968.

*Thailand*
NUECHTERLEIN, DONALD E. *Thailand and the Struggle for Southeast Asia*, Cornell University Press, 1965.
WILSON, DAVID A. *The United States and the Future of Thailand*, Praeger, 1970.

*Indochina*
RANDLE, ROBERT F. *Geneva 1954: The Settlement of the Indochinese War*, Princeton University Press, 1969.
DEVILLERS, PHILIPPE, and LACOUTURE, JEAN. *End of a War: Indochina, 1954*. Pall Mall Press, 1969.
KIRK, DONALD. *Wider War: The Struggle for Cambodia, Thailand, and Laos*, Praeger, 1971.
ZASLOFF, JOSEPH J. and GOODMAN, ALAN E. (eds). *Indochina in Conflict*, D. C. Heath & Co., 1972.

*Vietnam*
ZAGORIA, DONALD S. *Vietnam Triangle*, Pegasus, 1967.
KAHIN, GEORGE McT. and LEWIS, JOHN W. *The United States in Vietnam*, Dial Press, 1969.
The New York Times, *The Pentagon Papers*, Quadrangle Books, 1971.

*Laos*
ADAMS, NINA S. and McCOY, ALFRED W. (eds). *Laos: War and Revolution*, Harper and Row, 1970.
DOMMEN, ARTHUR J. *Conflict in Laos*, Praeger, 1971.

*Cambodia*
SMITH, ROGER. *Cambodia's Foreign Policy*, Cornell University Press, 1966.
LEIFER, MICHAEL. *Cambodia: The Search for Security*, Praeger, 1967.

*Malaysia/Singapore*
BOYCE, PETER. *Malaysia and Singapore in International Diplomacy*, Sydney University Press, 1968.
TILMAN, ROBERT O. 'Malaysian Foreign Policy: The Dilemmas of a Committed Neutral', *Public Policy*, Cambridge, 1967.
WILSON, DICK. *The Future Role of Singapore*, Oxford University Press, 1972.

*Indonesia*
FEITH, HERBERT. 'Dynamics of Guided Democracy' in *Indonesia*, Ruth T. McVey (ed.), HRAF Press, 1963.
SOEDJATMOKO. 'Indonesia and the World', Australian Outlook, 1967.
FEITH, HERBERT, and CASTLES, LANCE. *Indonesian Political Thinking 1945-1965*, Cornell University Press, 1970, Chapter XV.
WEINSTEIN, FRANKLIN B. 'Indonesia' in Wayne Wilcox, Leo E. Rose, and Gavin Boyd (eds), *Asia and the International System*, Winthrop, 1972.

*The Philippines*
MEYER, MILTON M. *A Diplomatic History of the Philippine Republic*, University of Hawaii Press, 1965.
GOLAY, FRANK H. (ed.). *The United States and the Philippines*, Prentice-Hall, 1966.

# INDEX

Acheson, Dean, 11
Algiers (Afro-Asian) Conference (1965), 61
Ali Sastroamidjojo, 33–4
Ananda Mahidon, King, 8
Anglo-Malayan Defence Agreement, 47
Anti-Fascist People's Freedom League, 12, 31
Asian Development Bank, 94
Asian Relations Conference (1947), 11
Association of Southeast Asia (ASA), 41–2, 48, 94
Association of Southeast Asian Nations (ASEAN), 62, 63, 67, 95, 99–100, 103, 108
Australia, 16, 47, 77, 103

Bao Dai, 9, 22, 24
Bandung Conference (1955), 20, 34, 41, 43, 50
Boun Oum, Prince, 39
Brezhnev, Leonid, 90
Britain, 6; and Burma, 12–13; and Malaya, 47; and Malaysia, 56, 60; and Thailand, 7–9
Brunei, 1, 57
Burma, 12–14, 29–32, 33, 70, 78, 85–6, 96–7; and China, 14, 29–32, 85–6, 96; and Soviet Union, 97; and Thailand, 70; and United States, 30–1; Communist Party of, 13, 85–6

Cairo Conference of Non-Aligned Countries (1964), 61
Calcutta Youth Conference (1948), 18
Cambodia, 22–3, 25–6, 35–7, 50–5, 68, 80–2, 86, 99, 103; and China, 35–7, 53, 86; and Democratic Republic of Vietnam, 53–4, 80–2; and Republic of Vietnam, 36, 52–3, 81–2; and Thailand, 36, 51–2; and United States, 36, 53, 80–2; National United Front of (FUNK), 82
Chiang Kai-shek, 6, 20
China, 6, 11, 13, 14, 19, 42, 77, 82–8, 96; and Burma, 29–32, 85–6; and Cambodia, 35–6, 81–2, 86; and Democratic Republic of Vietnam, 25, 46, 84–5; and Indonesia, 34, 85; and Laos, 84; and Thailand, 43
Chou En-lai, 31, 41, 43, 86
Christison, Lt General Philip, 15
Colombo Conference (1954), 19, 28
Colombo Plan, 94
Colonial International Order, 3–4
Cominform, 18, 88
Corregidor Affair, 63

d'Argenlieu, Admiral, 22
Diem, Ngo Dinh, 24, 44–5, 52, 75, 76

Economic Commission for Asia and the Far East (ECAFE), 93–4